CAREERS IN
HUMAN RESOURCE MANAGEMENT

Graeme Connelly

KOGAN PAGE

First published in 2000

Apart from any fair dealing for the purposes of research or private study, or criticism or review, as permitted under the Copyright, Designs and Patents Act 1988, this publication may only be reproduced, stored or transmitted, in any form or by any means, with the prior permission in writing of the publishers, or in the case of reprographic reproduction in accordance with the terms and licences issued by the CLA. Enquiries concerning reproduction outside these terms should be sent to the publishers at the undermentioned address:

Kogan Page Limited
120 Pentonville Road
London N1 9JN

© Kogan Page, 2000

British Library Cataloguing in Publication Data

A CIP record for this book is available from the British Library.

ISBN 0 7494 3221 7

Typeset by Kogan Page
Printed and bound in Great Britain by Clays Ltd, St Ives plc

Contents

Preface .... *iv*

1. Introduction 1
Is this the job for you?; Human resource management and personnel management; Professionalism; Careers and rewards; A typical HR professional

2. The organizations 7
Size; Sector

3. Occupational areas 13
Recruitment and selection; Human resource planning; Employee/industrial relations; Training and development; Equal opportunities; Health and safety; Reward, benefits and pensions; Specialization; Specialisms in HRM; Summary

4. Allied careers 41
Consultancy; The Law; Academia

5. Getting started 48
Top Tips for getting into HRM; Your current situation; Where to look; Your personal development plan

6. Qualifications 62
The requirement for qualifications or experience; Routes to qualification; The qualifications; The qualified HRM professional

7. The future of human resource management 75

8. Further information 79
Where to study; The Internet; Useful publications and further reading

9. Useful addresses 83

Index *93*

Preface

The personnel department in an organization may seem a little mysterious to the outsider. What *is* it that people in personnel do? It is clearer what trainers get up to. We know that there are training sessions organized at work and we may have been on some courses ourselves. We can also relate training to what goes on in the classroom at school. On the other hand, we rarely see the people in personnel. Apart from the important things like making sure that we have a contract and that we are paid on time, it is often unclear how personnel managers fill up the rest of their day.

This book aims to dispel some myths and expand on the real practice of personnel practitioners, trainers and developers. It aims to show how central the subject is to the running and success of any organization. On this basis, it is not some grey support function, but a complex, demanding yet accessible career that runs right to the top of any organization.

Human Resource Management is therefore a possible career at any stage of life. Whether you are still at school, returning to work or looking for it, or whether you want to change your career, there are ways of getting into the profession. This book looks at ways of doing this from each perspective.

1 Introduction

Is this the job for you?

- ❏ Do you enjoy helping people?
- ❏ Do you enjoy having many things on the go at the same time?
- ❏ Is constant contact with people important?
- ❏ Do you want a career that you can map out long in advance?

What about these questions?

- ❏ Is helping people not your top priority?
- ❏ Do you like to get stuck into the detail of one particular job at a time?
- ❏ Do you prefer to work on your own for most of the time?
- ❏ Do you want a varied career that you won't be able to predict a month in advance, never mind years?

Surprisingly, perhaps, if you have answered yes to some of either set of questions, then a career in Human Resource Management (HRM) might be for you.

A few more questions:

- ❏ Can you always keep confidential information to yourself?
- ❏ Are you good at arguing your point of view?
- ❏ Do you shy away from people if they talk personally?
- ❏ Do you think certain groups of people are naturally more talented?

If you answered 'no' to the first two questions or 'yes' to the last two questions, then HRM is probably not your best career choice.

Human resource management and personnel management

There are many views on whether there is a difference between Human Resource Management (HRM) and Personnel Management. In this book, they are considered as essentially interchangeable, covering all aspects of planning for, managing and developing the people in organizations. Whether the organization is a large multinational or a small charity, a local housing unit or a high-tech electronics manufacturing plant, the opportunities in HRM are vast. Someone, or a whole department, will be devoted to the overall management of the people in that organization.

HRM is used here also to encompass the training and development function, sometimes referred to as Human Resource Development (HRD). Some will argue that HRD is a completely separate function and, indeed, in many organizations this is so. In others there is a greater integration of HRM and HRD. Both approaches may be appropriate and will depend on the sort of organization – its history, function, position in the market place and many other factors. HRM is used here as a convenient catch-all phrase, rather than as any intent to subsume HRD into HRM.

Some will have come into HRM knowing that this was what they wanted to do. Others will have been asked to take on some part of HRM and gradually moved into it as they took up the many challenges that were open to them. Some will have come from school, worked perhaps in general administration, and have been asked to arrange training sessions for a group of staff. Others will have been working maybe in a production company or social work, had some line management responsibilities and decided to pursue the management of people further. Yet others might have gained a first degree in a general subject – psychology, history, geography or biology, perhaps – and wished to pursue a more vocational subject in order to enhance their career prospects. The avenues into HRM are as varied as the jobs themselves and as unique as the organizations in which you can work.

As an HR professional, you might cover a range of roles as a 'generalist':

- recruitment and selection;
- human resource planning;
- employee/industrial relations;
- training and development;
- equal opportunities;
- health and safety;
- reward, benefits and pensions.

You might also be more significantly involved in one or more of these roles as a specialist or move into key advisory roles in:

- international law;
- management development;
- organizational development;
- HRM software design/development.

Professionalism

Whether you eventually choose a generalist role, enjoying the variety of tasks and seeking to fit them together, or a specialist role, becoming deeply involved in one particular area of HRM, it is important that you can maintain standards of conduct that are seen to be fair. If you give someone a job because you believe that some groups of people are better suited to certain jobs than others, then you will be ignoring one of the cornerstones of professional behaviour – compliance with the law. However, professionalism goes even further. It goes without saying that you should behave in the best interests of the organization and the people it employs. What if someone in the organization wants you to do something unethical or even illegal?

HRM relies on a code of conduct in the same way that other professionals do – doctors, lawyers and accountants. This may be a personal ethical stance, one that you think any reasonable person would agree with. It may be guided by the various position statements made by the Chartered Institute of Personnel and Development (CIPD), a practitioner's institute concerned with enhancing the role of HRM and the people who specialize in it. With around 100,000 members it can be considered one of the largest representative professional bodies in the UK and the Republic of Ireland and can reasonably be thought of as the voice of HRM in these countries.

Careers and rewards

A barrister or advocate can expect a long period of training, pupillage, tenancy at chambers, maybe become a circuit judge, eventually taking silk, Queen's Counsel or Senior Counsel. Unlike many such traditional professions, HRM, with its variety of specialisms, has a less rigid career structure. As a result of the many roles an HR professional may take, the work can often seem to be a series of interlinked projects. Any one of these might lead to focusing on one area and being reappointed as the manager for that specialist area. From this, you might become the manager responsible for that area throughout the organization, worldwide. Perhaps, instead, you might choose to join a consultancy that sells precisely that specialism, or you might opt to remain a generalist, advising on the fit of the HR strategy with the business goals of the organization, leading from management to directorship.

Nevertheless, in more traditional companies, there are the standard levels of jobs in HRM, from HR or training clerk or assistant, through to HR or training officer, manager and director. A word of caution here: if you look at job advertisements in the newspapers, specialist magazines or the Internet, you will see a Training Assistant in one advertisement with a job description identical to that of a Training Manager in another organization. You will also see a Personnel Manager sought at the same salary as a Director of Human Resources elsewhere. What you are required to do, what experience you have and, perhaps, what qualifications you have, are more significant than the job title.

What you will see is that, in general, the reward packages are comparable with other professional appointments. The level of clerk or assistant is broadly that of an administration assistant; that of officer equivalent to an administrator or coordinator. The levels of manager and director, given the proviso stated above, will match those of manager and director of sales, benefits, production, housing or funding.

A typical HR professional

People from all backgrounds work in HRM. It is noticeable that slightly more women than men are employed as HR professionals. A higher than average level of black and Asian people work in some parts of the profession, for example in public service. However, this does not alter the composition of the HR workforce: it still can reflect the imbalances in organizations across the country. There *are* women contributing to the strategic success of businesses as HR managers; there *are* black directors of personnel; there *are* management development consultants who are Asian. As with any profession, it depends on the organization itself.

HRM is based on understanding skills and behaviour, rather than background or gender, as the source of success. So, it appears fair to say that the chances of developing your career based on what you do, rather than what school you went to, is greater. The Chartered Institute of Personnel and Development recommends that managing diversity (MD) underpins HR practice. This approach sees the differences between individuals as the additional possibilities available to the organization – and therefore something to be encouraged.

So, a typical HR professional looks like you or me, or anyone else. There is nothing typical about him or her. The variety of skills and abilities, talents and characteristics that someone may bring to the many possible jobs in so many different organizations, rules out the identikit personnel person. The following chapters will, by defining in more detail the possibilities for someone with ability and drive, underline the range of roles available and the diversity of the people required to carry them out.

2 The organizations

As there are differences between individual organizations and the jobs within them, is it possible to consider broad approaches in different sorts of organization? Is there a typical way of looking at HRM, depending on whether you work for the housing department in a northern municipal borough, a small, Dublin-based electronics firm or an international charity run outside a small west country town?

Size

As television advertising enjoys telling us, size matters. In organizations with fewer than 50 employees, it is rare for anyone to be designated personnel-, human resource- or training-anything. A small organization can rarely afford the possibility of dedicating anyone full-time to the task of forming and implementing personnel strategy – and would probably not wish to do so. Most organizational strategy will be formed by the managing director, chief executive officer – however they style themselves – with advice perhaps from a couple of trusted managers. How to deal with employees, whether recruiting, rewarding or firing them, is likely to be considered at the same time as the strategy itself. Indeed, in such organizations, strategy development is mostly seen in terms of the activities of the individuals to hand.

Unless you are one of these strategy-makers, then your involvement in HRM in a small organization is likely to be limited to instructions from the boss. At its most limited, it could be to

7

place a recruitment advertisement in a local newspaper and sift out patently unsuitable candidates. In other organizations, you might be asked to research possible approaches to staff appraisal and come up with some recommendations. The type of organization (manufacturing, service), sector (private, public, not-for-profit), external pressures (economic, competitive, legal) and the sorts of people at the head of the organization will also affect the approach to HRM.

Case Study

Jane *is Personal Assistant to the Managing Director.*

'I was involved in nursing for a number of years and slowly got pulled into administration as much as nursing. Once [my daughter] was at school, I really began to think of going back to work. With the sort of time I knew I would have to give to nursing, I decided to go for something in administration. Although I hadn't been working full-time since nursing, I had studied at the local library. They had free courses in computer skills. So I picked up the basics on word-processing and spreadsheets and ended up doing some part-time work for someone in the village who ran his business from home. When this job came up in a firm just down the road from where I live, it seemed too good to be true. I really had most of the experience they were after, I was ready for a full-time position, they were flexible about hours and it was good pay. The only thing was that I had never done personnel before and that was supposed to be part of the job.

Still, they took me on and I just started to pick it up – a bit like the part-time work I was doing before. When I arrived, I ended up writing my own acceptance letter offering myself my own job! I didn't quite manage to offer myself the salary I wanted, though. Anyway, I sorted out a system for recruiting and pulled everything together in files. Of course, before then, they were always losing CVs. Anyway [the managing director] asked me to start to choose the four best candidates. From that I was able to pin him down and said that we would need a job description if I was going to do that. He grumbled a bit but he could see the sense, even though he actually found it quite hard at the beginning. In the end we sit there and I keep asking him if they need to do this or that, until we have run out of ideas. He says he used to spend days seeing people before. I'm not surprised, if he didn't know what he was after in the first place.

Another thing I did was to help sort out the contracts. Well, I'm no expert in legal matters but when they gave me my contract, even I could see the problems with it. I could imagine some of the nurses getting a contract like that and rubbing their hands with glee. There were so many holes in it. I started coming up with suggestions and in the end we sent these with the old contract and some other suggestions to our solicitors. They passed it on to a firm that specializes in employment law and we've just introduced the new version. This employment law specialist now sends updates on changes in the law each month and I summarize the main points ready for the next revision of the contract.

I'm slowly taking on more of the personnel issues and I'm beginning to feel a bit overwhelmed – it just grows and grows. So, I've been thinking of going back into studying again, not that the boss knows yet. I've got to work out where and how – and how much. Then I'll have to think of a way of persuading him how valuable my studying would be to the firm.'

Sector

Traditions are sometimes specific to a particular organization. This firm has always shut down during the same two weeks every summer. Council housing in that particular borough has always been in short supply and so people do not last long in the housing department. Raising this particular charity's finance, now that it is part of the yearly, televised fund-raising exercise, is seen as glamorous, so people are always trying to 'defect' from other departments. As a result HR planning is so difficult that it is simply no longer done. Sometimes there are general characteristics that can be said of groups of organizations within the same sector, although, as with all generalizations, you will be able to think of many exceptions.

Private sector

Apart from the size of the business, there is also a standard distinction between those involved in manufacturing and those in service industries, such as retail outlets, engineering services or hotels and leisure complexes. Although there are far fewer firms involved in manufacturing nowadays, the sector is an important employer, often set up as the sole major local employer where previous industries have been allowed to die. If they are old, established manufacturing plants, they are likely to have particular traditions and ways of doing things that might be difficult to change quickly in times of threat: rigid job descriptions, significant training commitments, collective bargaining with many trade unions. However, these very things can also be seen as defences against new management imposing the latest fads onto the business and thereby using up resources the firm can scarcely afford.

If they are new, so-called 'greenfield' manufacturing plants then the emphasis might be on the flexibility of the work and the contract. You may have more direct involvement in making decisions about your work, greater opportunities for personal development and the possibility of team-working. Again, this may make for much wider experience and perhaps a more fulfilling sense of completing the job. On the other hand, career paths are less clear, you are more likely to be in a non-unionized environment and the flexibility might seem to be one-sided.

Service organizations may vary from small engineering organizations installing central heating equipment, to large finance organizations selling and servicing pensions, insurance and so on.

Public sector

The public sector has often been seen as more stick-in-the-mud, less glamorous and highly bureaucratic, with rules and regulations for everything from using the correct appraisal forms to requesting paper clips. Well, this might be true of certain areas of the public sector and it is reasonable to say that the private sector can often move forward faster, particularly for smaller organizations. However, with customer focus and quality of service now being considered as important as controlling costs, this is changing. Many local council responsibilities, for example cleaning or maintenance services, are provided by a separate organization, either directly or indirectly controlled by the council, and run as if they were private companies. Schools and hospitals have a similar approach.

Not-for-profit sector

This, the 'voluntary sector', used to be seen as an extension of the public sector. Worse, it was not only considered highly bureaucratic but seen as employing those people no one else wanted – well meaning but just not up to a proper job. This is certainly no longer the case.

The not-for-profit sector, particularly the major charities, have embraced all the techniques used in private business and require as high standards of employees as the most exacting of blue-chip companies.

Each sector has its attractions for the job seeker but it is for you to consider your own character and aspirations. Go back to the questions asked in the introduction and consider how your answers might fit with each of the sectors outlined in this chapter. Is there any particular sector that seems to stand out for you?

Case Study

Rizwan is a UK Assistant Personnel Manager in an international charity.

'I started out not really knowing what I wanted to do – I'd just followed the things I was good at in school and college and so ended up doing an HND in business and finance. Although I was good at maths, and thought I might go for accounting, I found I was more interested in the 'people side' – how organizations worked, their cultures and managing people.

I found a job in my local council, initially in the payroll department but there was an opening in the HR department for a personnel assistant and I was transferred. It was there I realized just how many different areas HRM really covers. In my first two years I dealt with standardizing appraisals across a whole department, contributed to a programme to reduce absenteeism and then concentrated on our recruitment and selection, looking at ways we could reduce bias in our advertising and recruitment procedures.

Although it was fun, it all seemed a bit faceless – I never really got to know people outside the HR department – and dealing with people was the reason I went into it. As a result of my concentrating on recruitment and selection, I moved to a recruitment agency, eventually interviewing and placing candidates in some really interesting companies – big city companies, television channels, really well known charities. Great money and I was dealing with lots of people, but just dealing with recruitment and selection seemed too limited for me. In the end, of course, I was trying to fill a job in this charity and I thought, "I'd like to do that". So, I spoke to the person I was dealing with at the charity and she arranged for me to be interviewed with the other candidates. I've been here five years and progressed to my current position with [the charity's] support. They are even supporting my studying with a loan and study leave. I eventually want to go on to do an MA in employment studies and look at the position of volunteers in organizations.'

So, the match of your own outlook to that of the organization may have something to do with the sort of sector you work in. It might not be just the sector, however. Even from this brief case study, the sort of work you can carry out and the level at which you do it are obviously extraordinarily varied. The next chapter will consider this variety in more detail.

3 Occupational areas

Apart from the main industry sectors, you might work at any level in the organization and concentrate on a particular field of HRM. A director specializing in employee relations will not do the same things as an HR administrator of employee relations. A management development specialist will have different skills and experiences from those of an IT training practitioner.

In larger organizations, as the last case study shows, there are significant opportunities for advancing in your HRM career, as well as moving from one specialist area to another, although, as with all professions, the greater your specialized knowledge, the more difficult the possibility of transition will be. The differences between someone who has spent the last five years analysing the skills needed for particular jobs and forecasting what the organization will require and someone experienced in devising training events focusing on personal communication are enormous. Think of an actuary, dealing with forecasting pension benefits, applying for a job as an occupational psychologist – there will be many more candidates with relevant experience who are likely to be considered for the job.

An HR 'generalist' is someone who is involved in a range of tasks and roles, perhaps dealing with a specific project in reviewing equal opportunities in the recruitment process for a time, while also maintaining the day-to-day running of the HR function. This generalist may then become involved in negotiations with unions about access to pensions, while monitoring the success of the first project. Although in some ways this can lead to a broadening of your career prospects, there is likely to be more competition from other generalists with your range of skills and experience. The decision to encompass a generalist or specialist role depends on how comfortable you feel about working strongly in a team and developing an understanding of how the organization works as a whole, or whether you prefer to know a particular subject in depth, become an acknowledged expert and fit this to a strategy within your particular field.

Looking at the various specialist HRM roles, as encountered in the introduction, can help to broaden an understanding of the different skills and abilities required and of the possibilities of integrating several of them in a more generalist capacity.

Recruitment and selection

Recruitment is the series of activities carried out to gain a pool of candidates who might match the organization's requirements for skills, knowledge, qualifications, experience, abilities and attributes. Recruitment may be for a specific job or may be to attract people likely to enhance the organization's success in a way that is moulded around the successful candidates.

Selection is the process of devising and carrying out methods of distinguishing people who match the organization's requirements most closely and contracting with them to work for that organization.

Both processes are seen by many as key elements in the success of an organization. In an increasingly customer-focused and quality-conscious environment, organizations in all sectors realize that the standard of applicants is critical. They also recognize that predicting candidates' future performance is crucial to the organization's own success. They are therefore spending increased amounts of time and money on attempting to devise the 'perfect' system for recruitment and selection.

In small organizations, the whole process might be carried out by one person, perhaps assisted by a general administrator to place the advertisements, collate the applications, send letters, arrange the interviews and confirm the appointment of successful candidates. Smaller organizations might work from an idea of what is to be carried out – the job description – and the sorts of skills that are needed to do it – the person specification. They might also set these down on paper and use them in the selection process.

In larger organizations, different tasks will be combined in the selection and recruitment process. A common misconception is that personnel deals with all of this. Given the amount of time and money invested in employees, it is unsurprising that integrating all these tasks is often the responsibility of the HR department. However, the marketing department might be involved in the design of any recruitment advertisements. Occupational psychologists might be contracted to consider the best profile of a successful candidate and carry out tests as a part of an assessment exercise. Trainers will be involved in explaining the interview process and developing an awareness of the skills needed for interviewing. Line managers will most often be a part of the interviewing process, sometimes the *only* person.

Case Study

Michelle is an HR Officer for a retail grocery chain.

'I've been working in HR for quite a few years now. Originally I worked in the north and was promoted to HR manager in a bank. Coming down to London meant that I had to look around for a bit. Even though in theory I'm back to being an HR officer, my responsibilities – and the pay – are at least as much. It's a generalist role and I have been mainly involved in opening up new stores in the south-east. In some ways it sounds a bit cocky, but you sit there and think, "Oh well, only two stores to open this quarter". And although you go through the same process – recruiting everyone, planning staffing levels and so on – each one has its own peculiarities. You find strange inconsistencies – in one store you have too few till staff available and two miles down the road you have far too many – and it's impossible to get them to shift from one store to the other.

Recently, I've been seconded to graduate recruitment. That's looking at potential candidates for our fast-track management programme. We have particular ties to two universities at the moment, although graduates from one of the two consistently drop out of the programme at a higher rate. We're trying to find out why and are looking at the same time at another university to approach. To be honest, I don't envy the graduate trainees. It really is a baptism of fire – coming from university with an idea that they will soon be running a store and the first thing they have to do is choose between working in the cold store or fruit and veg. One of the things I'm working on at the moment is how to get over to potential candidates exactly what is involved while still trying to sell [the company]. After all, there are a lot of other graduate recruitment schemes with companies that don't make you spend your first week up to your elbows in frozen fish.

One of the first things I did was to survey the current graduate trainees and, if I could trace them, any who had dropped out. Funnily enough, it isn't the fact that they have to get stuck in at the bottom that gets to them – although they do say it's a bit of a shock. More often, it's the antagonism from the existing department managers, who have worked their way through the system and are upset that these youngsters, fresh from college, have a chance that they never had. I'm thinking at the moment how we can turn this round: why don't existing staff have a fast-track opportunity, too?'

Nevertheless, the HR professionals first have had to consider what skills, knowledge and abilities are required, how these relate to the jobs to be carried out and how best to put these together – job design. They will also have to consider what these characteristics and responsibilities are worth – job evaluation. From this, a job description and person specification can be developed. Then they will have to consider how to attract the best, rather than the widest, pool of candidates. Is the job highly specialized? Do local people have the skills? Advertising in a regional paper might be sufficient or the vacancy might have to be placed in a specialist magazine. Petrochemical analysts, music therapists or urban planners will all look in different newspapers and magazines. Potential candidates might go to recruitment agencies that concentrate on attracting and placing people in specific industries or in particular professions. They might consider only organizations that advertise through their Web site.

All this is needed before seeing one CV or application form. The selection process involves professional judgement long before a candidate applies. Decisions need to be made about what will be required from the candidate in order to shortlist those who will be invited to interview, choosing whether to limit it to a CV and letter, an application form, copies of qualifications or references. Judgement is involved too in the shortlisting process, just as in the interview itself. There may be the option of using an assessment centre, where candidates will be asked to carry out a range of tasks and exercises that can match individuals' skills and characteristics to a predetermined profile of the ideal candidate. This is supposed to remove the potential for bias in the selection process. Discrimination, based on the requirements of the job, is necessary. Determining if someone has the skills, knowledge and abilities set out in the person specification is a part of the selection process. However, discrimination based on the personal beliefs of an interviewer, that particular groups of people have better or worse skills just because they belong to that group, is ethically unacceptable and reduces the pool of candidates from which the organization can select.

There are probably as many recruitment and selection schemes as there are organizations. However, they all demand, to a degree, a variety of skills from the HR professional: analytical skills in designing jobs and comparative financial skills in evaluating them. They also require communications skills in devising attractive job descriptions and advertisements, investigative skills in shortlisting and interviewing and a strong personal ethical code.

Human resource planning

Once upon a time, there used to be 'manpower planning', a supposedly rational, planned approach to finding out how many people and what skills would be required in each department. If the organization was expanding or contracting, the questions would be, 'By how much?' 'Who was in line for promotion and who was leaving for new jobs or well-earned retirement?' As the term betrays, such an old-fashioned approach did not appreciate the realities of organizations. It did not accept that employers would be happy to say that a job is no longer for life. In response, employees would see their skills and experience as tradable commodities and actively seek new opportunities in the job market. It did not consider the rapidity of change in commercial and public life either: contracts would be lost and new competitors would march in to take a company's previously stable market share. Political and legal upheavals meant changes to employees' rights and entitlements, and organizations amalgamated, merged or were taken over. A different approach was needed.

Human Resource Planning (HRP) has the same concerns but can recognize firstly the limitations of such a rational, long-term planning exercise. It also acknowledges the importance of a flexible and diverse workforce, with the continuous development of additional skills in the workplace. This means that forecasting is less of an exact science but still takes on some of the analytical approaches to employment levels in the organization. It therefore attempts to rely as much on the development and advancement of each employee as the selection of new blood. Training professionals may be involved to identify these possibilities in conjunction with generalist HR workers who will also consider reward as a part of managing people's careers.

Case Study

Padhraig is an HR administrator in a large recruitment consultancy.

'With so many consultants coming and going, it always seemed a strange idea that I'd be looking at planning the HR for the coming period – our three-year plan. We have a core of consultants who have been here some time but there's also a steady stream of consultants who will chase commission – here or elsewhere. I thought it would be impossible. I'd been involved with quite a few projects before in job analysis – interviewing current employees using critical incident technique [one of a range of analytic processes for charting the tasks carried out and skills required] – and had set up the new recruitment procedures. So when this project came up, with the possibility of linking all of that with appraisals and the training department, I was really keen.

It's been hard work but I've been involved with every department and have talked to every senior manager in [the business]. With the job analysis projects I was already primed but [the] training [department]'s been really supportive. We're particularly keen to reduce the [amount we] spend on recruitment and so we've been looking at broadening the training to cover our administration and marketing staff. That way, we should – more or less – be able to fill our junior- to middle-ranking positions. I'm also talking to [the training department] about management development possibilities so that we have people staying on for the more senior posts.

The consultants are still a problem. I don't see offering them endlessly increasing commission bonuses as the way forward. Our competitors will still try and offer more. Instead, I'm looking at finding ways of increasing their status – giving them key clients as their sole responsibility, for permanent and temporary staff, that sort of thing. At the moment they are always allocated to senior consultants in the two divisions – permanent and temporary. That's going to be quite a battle, trying to break down the barriers between those. If it works it will be worth it, though. It's still not really as clear as I would like it to be, particularly in terms of budgets, and I'm not sure it ever will be as clear as finance would like it, but I'm determined they will see a difference. And if they approve, I'll be knocking on their door come appraisal time.'

HRP is an all-encompassing part of HRM, involving project planning, interviewing and budgeting. It always envisages new possibilities for the development of the workforce and gaining allies to carry through each project. It relies on self-sufficiency and the ability to encourage others to move forward in ways that might or might not be anticipated.

Employee/industrial relations

Simply put, there are two schools of thought regarding communication, consultation and negotiation with employees. One would say that the only way to communicate with employees is on an individual basis. Through this, it is argued, the company can gain greater commitment and therefore greater flexibility from its employees. The other argues that established methods using elected representatives of broad groups of employees are more acceptable to employees and therefore decisions made in conjunction with those representatives are likely to gain the support of a majority of employees.

The first, employee relations, prefers to involve employees directly in the workplace, focusing on problem-solving teams and a greater fluidity of roles and expectations. Union representation is likely to be discouraged as irrelevant or antagonistic and so consultation forums rather than bargaining rounds are likely to be the focus of HR professionals. They will also have to consider the involvement of employees in the workplace through, for example, setting up focus groups on quality, the training and development resulting from that, and the evaluation of individuals' contributions to the organization's success.

Most often seen in the private and, particularly, the service sectors, the employee relations approach will encourage people to identify themselves strongly with the corporate culture, so it might appeal to those who feel they want to belong, who feel that their contribution will be best recognized on an individual basis. However, some employees are likely to be seen as more important to the organization's success than others. As a result HR professionals can encounter problems in communicating with and gaining commitment from part-timers, home- and shift-workers. Successful employees are likely to be committed to their careers rather than to the organization and therefore may cause problems for HRP, suddenly leaving for more lucrative jobs or for greater status.

Case Study

Paul is an HR Manager in Employee Relations in a large financial institution.

'This week has been great fun: the announcement that the takeover really is going to happen has just about capped everything. In some ways staff are more relieved now that the uncertainty has been taken away even though it's quite clear that there will be significant job losses as a result... I'd better explain what it is I do, or rather, what I don't. People always imagine with my job title that I'm constantly locked away in smoke-filled rooms doing battle with the trade unions, putting down the brothers and maintaining the forces of capitalism. It's true, we do have an internal staff association covering the majority of staff, as well as recognition of two unions for support staff and our customer services division, which are run as devolved units. But formal negotiation with any of them is not a part of my job. Of course I have close contact with staff representatives and convenors. It's important to discuss possibilities with them, float ideas and get feedback. I need to know what sort of resistance we could encounter for any strategies the company is considering. They're good at trying to block things initially but generally we get on. Mostly something can be sorted out. Now, though, it looks like a lot of that is about to disappear. Of course with the takeover looming, it has already become frosty, with minimal constructive discussion going on. It is frustrating – it takes a long time to develop relationships that you feel actually benefit everyone – the company and the employees. At the same time, I suppose the change is necessary. Our performance [in the sector] has been slipping for some time and I could foresee a much tougher takeover proposal coming from the Pacific Rim.

That's only part of my job, although it's obviously going to be a significant one for a while. Unusually, we have quite a mix of direct and indirect relations with staff [consultation between management and employees as well as with their representatives]. A significant proportion of my time has been about developing stronger communication links directly with the employees. So we have a system of team briefing, where each managerial and supervisory level comes together with one of their managers so that major changes and announcements can be discussed. This carries on all the way through the company, so that in theory everyone has had the chance to talk about whatever direction senior management has decided we should go. This also means, again in theory, that everyone has discussed the same thing. It doesn't quite work like that but it's still reasonably successful. In the lead up to this takeover, rumours have been flying around, as you would expect. Team briefing has at least helped to curb the wilder excesses of gossip that have been floating around.'

The second school of thought, industrial relations, may involve negotiations with one or a number of unions, or indeed a company employees' forum. The negotiations themselves might be limited to working conditions – the number of people working in a particular office, the provision of VDU filter screens. Negotiations might consider wage and productivity deals, training provision and the value of 'portable skills' or pension rights and contributions. They might be with the organization alone or as a part of an employers' group, for example with all electricians. They might be local negotiations, for example with certain public sector employees. The basis for approaching employees through representatives is seen as the ease with which communications are organized. It is also to gain greater commitment from employees to conditions negotiated on their behalf by professionals with the collective power of the union's members behind them. The rationale is, of course, that this can gain more than the limited power of the individual in negotiation. For the HR professional, of course, this can also limit the possibility of change, the response to external pressures on the organization and restrict the ability to deal with an individual employee's under-productivity or poor performance.

Clearly, there are many approaches in organizations that combine elements of the two. Equally clearly, they demand quite different skills from the HR professional. Employee relations asks for someone who can institute strong communication channels throughout the organization, someone who is able to develop a strong corporate message and gain measurable levels of commitment and involvement from employees. Industrial relations, on the other hand, will often require a forceful negotiator with a wide grasp of the legal background to those negotiations. As a result, someone considering this element of HRM is more likely to have had a career outside the profession, perhaps originally as a union convenor, from an involvement in the legal profession, or in other areas of significant negotiations.

Training and development

Until recently, training and development (T&D) was seen as a career and practice distinct from HRM. In larger companies, T&D and HRM would often act in different departments, corresponding with one another as was felt necessary. There was a traditional antipathy, reinforced by the relative pay differences between comparative jobs – training and development professionals were consistently paid less. Since a recognition of the value of the skills and abilities of employees to the organization and the importance of developing new skills in the light of organizational change, this relationship has altered. Many organizations now have an integrated HRM and T&D department, understanding that T&D is central to the success of all the elements of HRM that are covered in this book. Other organizations will retain the distinctions but ensure the compatibility of strategy and practice. With this has come a change in the status and the reward of T&D professionals and a complementary understanding of the ability of integrated T&D initiatives to have an impact on the success of organizations.

T&D professionals will argue, for example, that a workforce that has the skills to carry out its jobs is likely to be more satisfied and motivated. This, in turn, should lead to employees remaining longer with the organization, particularly if they are involved in a continuous process of updating their skills. As a result, this makes HRP easier, reduces the costs of recruitment and alleviates the problems of having new workers without the skills or knowledge of the organization. In an age where employees understand that they are as marketable as the skills, abilities and experience that they possess, an organization that fuels the enhancement of these may benefit from increased performance, flexibility and commitment.

To consider the activities and characteristics of the T&D professional, it is first important to understand what the terms 'training' and 'development' mean. Training is considered to be job- or organization-focused, with a recognizable, short-term effect. It will therefore be used in induction – the initial training gained on joining an organization – or in changing or accepting new roles. Development, although often initiated or assisted by the organization, concentrates on the individual and the development of his or her potential over the long-term. Successful development is the responsibility of the individual and personal development programmes are likely to form a part of the career progression of employees, particularly in management. Someone involved specifically in the design and delivery of development programmes will often specialize in this element of the learning process alone. However, training professionals may develop and present many different types of training events. In either case, the importance of presentation, persuasiveness, something of being on the stage, will be necessary to the T&D professional. As with stage performers, however, good preparation and focused rehearsal are vital to the success of the training event or development programme. The show is only one part of the job.

In order to consider T&D in any strategic sense, then the results of HRP – job analysis and design – will need to be taken into account. These will feed into an analysis of the training needs of the organization, together with any new requirements – for example a new research and development unit, expanding marketing into Europe, reorganizing the North American operation, or reducing the workforce in France and relocating to Korea. The performance of existing employees must be appraised and future training needs ascertained. All of this will form a part of a training needs plan. Only then can training programmes be considered, developed, planned and presented.

Even once the training and development programmes have been completed that is not the end of it. Evaluating success, some would say the most difficult part of the T&D professional's remit, needs to be assessed through the same mechanisms: is there a reduced turnover of staff, greater productivity, reduced health and safety incidents, fewer quality problems or customer complaints?

Although the T&D practitioner's job is not necessarily desk-bound, planning and evaluation are key to her or his own success and that of the organization. So, clear analytical skills, a knowledge of the subject and, most importantly, an ability to communicate clearly and persuasively are all bound into the role of the T&D professional. As someone specifically involved in development, rather than training, then the integration with HRM is going to be even more intertwined. A knowledge of the interrelationships of the profession will again be a key to the success of the development programmes that have been put in place. In both instances, although a knowledge of the subjects being taught or discussed will be important, it is likely that a training professional will produce better results than those of an expert brought in to impart their knowledge of a particular subject. Once the research and the final rehearsals are complete, the show rests on the trainer's own individual talents.

Case Study

Gene is a Training Officer for an independent training group.

'I worked in all sorts of jobs before moving into training. Not that you could just turn up and say, "I want to be a trainer". I suppose I realized the connection between what I thought I was doing – initially telesales and then supervising and managing sales people – and training. I cottoned on to the fact that I enjoyed seeing the results of the coaching work: I could always enthuse people and get them to see a different way of doing things. Perhaps it's a result of my acting work in the past.

Anyway, I applied for a training administrator's job and reasonably quickly persuaded them to give me a try in active training. Not that they let me near a customer for ages. I had to enrol for the CIPD [qualification] and, as a part of that, had to develop a training programme for another organization. [My company] took that on board and, with the senior training officer, we developed a complete training course. On the back of that, I sat in and helped with other courses in personal communication and presentation and quite a few simulations. I began to take an active part in the course presentations.

Nowadays, I'm developing and presenting courses in sales techniques but I have moved more into personal skills – how comfortable people feel with other people's aggression and how to deal with it, that sort of thing. The feedback is terrific. I had one guy who seemed to change in front of us over the course of three days. He was so timid in the beginning and just so strong by the end. In some ways it would be good to find out more, be part of where he was working, and see what changes happened as a result. Something must have happened, though, because we have repeat bookings from that company.'

Equal opportunities

There has been a recognition for decades, of evidence that identified groups of people are disadvantaged in the workplace, whether from blatant prejudice, or from badly thought out procedures that give dominant groups an advantage. Employment law enacted over the last 50 years has been concerned with attempts to eradicate discrimination against people on the basis of their disablement, gender, ethnicity or religion. Further judgements in the European courts have continued to refine understandings of discrimination regarding these groups and others, for example concerning sexual orientation.

For some time, approaches to equal opportunities (EO) in organizations have been anything from a denial that there might be any problems at all, to a wholehearted embracing of the legal requirements, with some organizations welcoming groups not covered by specific legislation. Some organizations, for example, set out clear guidelines to deter discrimination based on the age of an applicant or employee.

In some organizations there is a specified equal opportunities practitioner, charged with ensuring compliance with the legislation. This may take the form of a review of all legislation and a survey of the population from which the organization draws its employees. The practitioner will then consider the employment procedures and the ways that people are managed. The possibility of designing jobs or application requirements that are discriminatory needs to be examined. Demanding that candidates are above a certain height, for example, may discriminate against certain ethnic groups. Similar conditions or procedures might occur throughout the employment process – in performance appraisals, pay awards, recommendations for promotion, access to training and severity of discipline.

However, it is not just paper processes and statistics that can ensure discrimination but conscious or unconscious bias or prejudice in individuals. So, equal opportunities practitioners will often work closely with the training and development department. The aim may not be to alter employees' attitudes, merely to ensure that their behaviour does not have a discriminatory effect. They will also need to consider how each of the HRM processes can be set up so that individuals' biases might be excluded or curtailed. In performance appraisals, supervisors or managers might not simply allocate a grade to an employee's standard of performance over the last year. They might grade against specific evidence and employees might appeal against the judgement. A more formal process might replace recruiting people by word of mouth. A manufacturing firm with all men on the shop floor is likely, by word of mouth, to employ current employees' mates. Many people choose friends who are similar to them and so the firm is likely to employ more men, ignoring a larger pool of candidates, some of whom might bring greater or different talents to the company.

Case Study

Buki is an Equal Opportunities Officer for a large security firm.

'I took this job nearly two years ago. I knew it would be a challenge but I thought I could really make a change. Well, we certainly have changed! Recruitment, for example, was just a mess – always a scramble when we got a new contract and we would take almost anyone on that anyone had ever heard of. Someone had worked with someone and had heard that he had just left the army (we get a lot of people from the services and police) so we took him on. It was almost a passport to a job, no questions asked.

Of course, much of our major work is government or council contract work and they demanded evidence of our equal opportunities policy. I'm under no illusions about why I was taken on – without an EO policy, they'll not get the contract – but I thought this would be to my advantage: I consistently have the argument at the back of everyone's mind – if you don't operate the EO policy, then no contract and no money.

I'll give you an example of how things were when I started. I suppose I was a bit naive. I'd come from working in a local council, developing quite cutting-edge stuff on equal opportunities and managing diversity. My first project was agreed as recruitment and selection. We'd had huge staff turnover, which isn't unusual in security, but there was a significant amount of complaints from clients, about people sleeping on the job, being abusive or plainly on the fiddle. In [the council] I was used to interviewers asking a set list of questions and not varying them, otherwise their attitudes might start swaying the candidates' answers. Here, when I sat in on the interviews, it was more of a chat, to see whether they liked the same football team! Now, when I was working in Scotland, that could be almost a code for asking about your religious beliefs.

Part of the EO policy the company agreed to was the formalizing of selection interviews. The managers didn't exactly jump for joy, of course, and the training department and I spent quite a long time devising courses and learning events. They're beginning to come around, though, as they realize that they don't have to spend a large part of their day fending off irate clients.'

The term 'managing diversity' (MD) that is used in the case study adopts a different approach to the idea of equality of opportunity. To begin with, advocates of MD argue that it is clear that EO has not worked. There is clear evidence that, despite legislation in place for decades, some groups are still disadvantaged.

Whereas EO takes its cue from legislation and an understanding of disadvantaged groups of people, proponents of MD see individuals' differences as opportunities to be harnessed and used to the advantage of the organization. The focus is on each individual's skills, characteristics and abilities, how to enhance them in the light of their experience and how best to use them to carry out their job.

For the HR practitioner, this means a much more long-term objective and a shift from simple training to development. He or she will have to focus more on the development of managers' skills, rather than on gaining people's compliance through training sessions that teach them the limits of acceptable behaviour. The practitioner will also have to build a case for investing time and money over a long period to adopt such an approach and will therefore have to develop ways of costing and measuring the specific benefits derived from it. They will need a broad range of interrelated business skills, from finance and statistical analysis through approaches to development, to long-term project management. They must also have the ability to persuade others of the business case for equality of opportunity.

Health and safety

The HR practitioner may be involved in areas of identifying, remedying and preventing disease or injury in the workplace. Comprehensive legislation and local agreement govern all of this, for example with union and health and safety representatives as well as occupational health workers. This will, of course, vary from organization to organization. An office-based charity is likely to be concerned primarily with ergonomics, the suitability of desks and chairs for the size of the people using them, equipment such as the glare from VDU screens and adequate fire precautions and exits. A supermarket must also take into account such concerns as the lifting of heavy boxes and working in cold stores as well as hygiene for both its employees and customers. A plant manufacturing electronic chips for telecommunications and computer use may have to consider the use of protective clothing, ventilation and the control of known carcinogens in use.

Regardless of the size or function of the organization, there are standard approaches to health and safety (H&S) that must be followed. Potential hazards in the workplace must be analysed. Policies and procedures for dealing with those hazards and reporting their occurrence must be drawn up. Methods of eliminating or reducing hazards to an acceptable level have to be defined. Finally the recommendations must be carried out and performance against the set standards regularly evaluated. Again, there is a link between the prevention of ill-health and accidents and T&D. This may simply consist of training for new employees during their induction period in the use of fire-fighting equipment or the requirement to take regular breaks from staring and typing at a computer screen. It will involve significant initial training and certification, for example in the petrochemical industries. Alternatively, it could involve sessions so that managers can develop an awareness of H&S regulations and issues as a part of the implementation of a new H&S policy.

A growing concern in organizations, partly due to well-publicized industrial tribunal cases, is that of unacceptable and avoidable stress at work. There are many possible causes: the design of the job places too many demands on the individual, a manager or colleague may single out and bully an employee, the job itself might demand that someone is working in a violent or highly aggressive environment. In each case, it is the responsibility of the organization and its structures of dealing with H&S, including the H&S practitioner, to look for ways of alleviating such stress, whether it is caused by the work itself or employees' colleagues or clients. All of this requires a methodical approach, creativity in foreseeing potential problems and ways of dealing with them and a versatility of approach: to be able to encourage involvement when appropriate but also to be a hard negotiator when necessary.

Reward, benefits and pensions

When we go to work, whatever the organization, we do so in return for money – pay, commission or bonuses. We expect reasonable treatment from employers and those who offer us work and so expect paid time off. Employers should accept that we may be ill from time to time. To attract us into the organization, they can offer additional ways of recognizing that we are human beings with a wide variety of interests and needs. There could be many options on offer: membership of sports clubs, subsidized meals, reasonable accommodation if we go on training courses or attend conferences, share options or even use of the company jet! In foreseeing a time when we no longer wish to work, we want adequate provision to enjoy our retirement in some comfort and seek organizations that can help us in planning and paying for this.

However, this is not the only reason most of us go to work. A sense of belonging to something, of enjoying being and working with others is a necessary part of our gaining satisfaction in the workplace. Having sudden challenges thrust upon us and resolving them, gaining recognition of our achievements, and learning and growing from all this, is important to us. In that sense, pay is too narrow a definition of how we are compensated for giving our time. Reward may at least attempt to encompass this understanding. On this basis, the HR professional is dealing with far more than methods of evaluating how much a job is worth and how much people should be given in the annual pay review – if there is one.

The remit of HR professionals involved in reward and benefit is wide. They must think about the systems of rewarding individuals and teams for particular effort, the fairness of performance appraisal and the management style in the organization. They must also consider how training is allocated and personal development is encouraged, as well as how employees can be motivated. So, there is a move beyond acting as payroll managers and administrators. Reward is seen as another way the organization can manage its employees and get the best from them, as long as it is integrated with the other tools of HRM that have been discussed.

HR practitioners dealing with reward can therefore be involved in a complex pattern of policies, strategies and processes. This means that they can be a part of senior management, developing the organization's own strategies and gaining an understanding of the ways by which people are rewarded. They can also consider the relationship of team-work and individual reward – how jobs are designed and interrelate. At a different level, it may be necessary to devise a system of rewarding individuals on the basis of their competence in carrying out a particular task. This is a complex project that demands developing a list of competencies required for the task, deciding how much these are worth, and considering the reward options available. Do you award money, status or additional benefits? Is this awarded only on completion? How is the employee encouraged to develop the competency –

Occupational areas

through training or coaching by his or her manager? All of these must be considered before the HR practitioner can decide how to implement the system or evaluate its success.

Case Study

Alex is an HR Manager for a housing association.

'It's difficult, this reward business. There seem to be so many different ideas, different demands that pull you in opposite directions, the more you think about it. Most of my time I've spent as a generalist. I was involved in developing rating scales for appraisals that would eventually channel through to the pay review, and I researched and put together our cafeteria package of benefits that we could offer to our managerial staff – that's a list of benefits that they can choose from, each one costed out and allocated a number of points. They can then use their points – the more senior the manager, the more points – a bit like a supermarket loyalty card, really. So, they can choose not to have a company car and put the money into their pension or take up the loan for an annual travel pass and take an additional three days annual leave.

Apart from this, I hadn't really been involved much in the reward side. Now, though, I've become more or less reward manager. My major concern at the moment is that non-managerial staff have been taken on over the years in different locations throughout the country by managers who could more or less set their own conditions, including pay. We have so many different contracts and rates of pay, I'd say we're employing at least two more payroll people than we really need. It's not as though they are dealing with huge variations from month to month – non-managerial staff don't have an option of cafeteria benefits. Well, not yet, anyway.

So, even before starting to think about what sort of unified pay system we need, we have to trawl through all the employees' conditions and see if some have significantly different job descriptions, or different hours, even different entitlement to paid sick leave. Once that's completed, we have to consider how we are going to get agreement from all of these people to the changes. After all, you can't just send everyone a letter and tell them that they are working for less or that you're going to make them work five hours a week more for the same pay. Of course, unionized staff do have standard contracts and terms but we deal with five of them and, of course, bargaining has been done with each individually, and there are discrepancies there too. That should be fun.

Only once I have a real idea of the size of the changes necessary, then I can start to think of the general approach to what we are going to replace it all with. I'm in favour of moving to competency-based training and reward but that will just add to the enormity of the task. Just think, suddenly we've got to go through a whole job analysis exercise from the perspective of competencies and evaluate all of them. That will involve the training department in some hefty work as well. The more I think about it, the bigger the project becomes. It's funny, really: although I'm being asked to be more of a specialist, the more it's pushing me back into being a generalist.'

So, the integration of tasks in this, as with the other elements of HRM, is a key to the successful implementation of reward strategies. Here, how to put the reward system in place and how to evaluate whether it has been successful have not even been mentioned. A change of system will require careful negotiation, either individually through employees' line managers, or collectively, through representatives or union negotiators. This may require compromise and a revision of original plans, which may also involve altering the direction of the strategy, its implementation or its evaluation. This last activity must also be built into the reward system. After all, you are there to gain greater motivation and commitment, possibly through a more flexible approach to working in terms of hours and functions.

Specialization

This entire chapter has so far considered the various elements of HRM and the tasks that the HR professional might be called upon to carry out. However, as can be seen, the integration of each element with the others, as well as with the goals of the organization, has been paramount. In larger organizations and specialist consultancies some HR professionals choose to focus on one or more areas in much greater depth. They can then call upon others' expertise at the same level, either as a specific project or as part of a team of HR specialists. Even so, an awareness of how activity in one sphere will affect another area, or will require others' involvement, will be the key to the successful implementation of any plan. It will also affect how the specialist is seen. Specialists buried in the minutiae of their chosen field, who disregard or do not know the impact of their work on others, are likely to be under-employed specialists.

Take, for example, the case of Alex, who, in attempting to standardize reward for non-managerial employees, began to realize how much larger the project was than he originally thought it was going to be. He started by approaching the project from one point of view – competency-based training and reward. This is where each of the activities required to carry out a particular job is defined in terms of what can actually be seen. As a result of this approach he would have had no choice but to change his plan at some time or another. He could have seen the project as a tidying-up exercise and just listed the differences between each of the employees' terms and conditions. Then all he would have had to do is think of a compromise that would be acceptable to staff and management. However, he would still have had to think of a way to stop the managers drifting back into offering different terms at the selection stage. He would also have had to consider ways of halting this drift when the managers were appraising employees for any annual pay review.

In identifying the different requirements of the project, he has also realized how important union negotiation, the training department and the managers themselves will be to its success. He can involve key personnel in each of these fields from an early stage and gain their commitment to the project. Otherwise he could risk the possibility of their feeling excluded and trying to block it. As experts in their own field, they may be able to offer alternative approaches or simplify the process. The training department might inform him that they have a plan to introduce particular National Vocational Qualifications (NVQs) and so have already carried out the programme of job analysis. He might be told that the unions had already brought up the discrepancies in terms and conditions between various groups of workers and that they were actively seeking some way of resolving this. This would mean that negotiations could be held with the active support of the unions for change.

Specialization in each of the HRM areas outlined is feasible and may at any time require groups of HR specialists becoming involved with other specialists in their field. This may happen with other HR specialists or with people from outside HRM. At different times you might see projects using HR planners with recruitment specialists or reward specialists with tax advisers. Health and safety specialists may well need to work with legal experts. Trainers and recruiters may seek the advice of occupational psychologists. Specialization in this sense will tend to mean dealing with that particular area of HR at a managerial rather than functional level. An HR administrator involved in setting up a computerized recruitment system possesses certain skills and knowledge. However, most of the skills, if not the knowledge, will be seen as transferable to other HR tasks. A senior union negotiator, with a reasonably comprehensive knowledge of industrial and contract law, is more likely to be sought out precisely for her or his expertise. He or she would be unable to move into some other fields, such as HRP, although there would be the possibility of specializing further in health and safety, for example. Alternatively, someone in this position could use the particular skills of planning, negotiation and breadth of legal knowledge to move into a general managerial role outside that of HRM.

There are many variations of the areas of HRM described above. HR specialists might be engaged as direct employees of an organization on a contract basis for a particular project. Small firms do not need full-time experts in such fields and certainly cannot afford them. Even larger organizations will choose to buy in such expertise when necessary. These specialists might also be brought in as consultants, either on a self-employed basis or as a part of a consultancy firm. The largest of these firms will have specialists in the complete range of organizational and management solutions. They will have worked not only in their chosen subject but also in a range of industries or sectors similar to the organization requiring their skills. They might have spent some time in their career advising on international law, management and organizational development or HRM software design. However, they will also have advised in these capacities within a further specialized field: the housing sector, retail management or small business development, for example.

Smaller agencies or groups of consultants will often focus on particular groups of services. There are many organizations that focus their business on providing NVQ assessment and assisting organizations gaining accreditation as an Investor in People (IIP).

They will advise on the link of targeted training to the aims of the organization, drawing up a training plan and either delivering some of the training or searching for the best training providers. Perhaps the best-known specialist agencies are the recruitment agencies. These may focus on working in a particular sector, for example health care workers. They are likely to provide permanent and temporary staff as well as a nurse 'bank'. Others may concentrate on providing potential administration and secretarial staff. Professional search agencies – 'headhunters' – seek to trace and attract key senior workers in particular industries or sectors away from their current jobs into those of their clients.

Specialisms in HRM

Management development

Not simply training for managers, management development embraces the idea that management is a complex role, often concerned with intangibles, such as creativity or persuasiveness. While not separate from training, it also assumes, as its name suggests, that management learning is ongoing and is best experienced, challenged and rethought in the context of work itself. A part of the process is also identifying the likely future development of particular managers and fitting that into the career planning of those managers and it is therefore allied to human resource planning. As managers are tasked with developing and implementing the business strategy, management development specialists will have to consider what these strategies are and how they link together. They will have to come up with proposals for management development that are accepted by those managers and gain the organization's agreement as to how these will be supported. Whether the organization chooses self-development or coaching will depend on the sort of organization and whether the focus is on existing managers or graduate trainees on a fast-track programme – so-called 'high fliers'.

Case Study

Joan is an HRD Manager in an investment bank.

'Some time ago I decided to move from straightforward skills training into management development, which is actually easier said than done. It really is quite different in many ways. In training there is obviously the high throughput of delegates and you have a chance to review the delivery of training courses you have repeated a number of times. With management development, you often have only one chance. If it doesn't go well, then you don't have the possibility of repeating it and getting better through repetition. I suppose my learning therefore mirrors more the development the managers undertake. It's more reflective, looking at what was good, what wasn't and searching for alternative approaches in the circumstances.

At [the bank] my remit is greater than just researching and implementing the management development programme. After all, HRD is about integration – with other HRD strategies, with HRM and, particularly with the management development, with the business strategy. Like many banks at the moment, we have to be alive to the possibility of merger and this is certainly on the cards. Managers can get a bit gung-ho in such an environment and it sometimes feels like they take 'learning by doing' a bit too far. It's then that the cohesion of the management team really comes under threat and we have to think fast in order to keep the session focused. Recently we spent one session getting nowhere. A couple of the managers had recently negotiated the acquisition of a small but quite important far-eastern institution. They brought this into the session a bit like a cat dumps next door's canary on your doorstep and then looks pleased with itself. The stink lingers for ages and they wouldn't drop the subject. In the end, we decided to concentrate on what they did to negotiate the deal – pull apart how they went about it and note where certain skills were used and how. When another manager piped up with a question about what would have happened in a certain situation, it became obvious that they hadn't planned for it. They were slightly humbled but agreed that they had gained something by the end of the session.'

Organizational development

In some workplaces, organizational development (OD) is a label for what is little more than management development. As can be seen from the case study above, management development focuses on individuals within the organization and how their development can contribute over time to the success of the organization. OD, on the other hand, while likely to encompass management development, is concerned with how the organization is constructed. It looks at what the assumptions are, what is done and how the organization deals with the involvement of employees. It considers planning, communication and conflict over time and in reaction to uncontrollable events.

The organization might have to deal with sudden, major competition from abroad or a merger with an organization that has a completely different culture. This can therefore be seen as an approach to change management. It must therefore understand the role of teams in the organization, how individuals work within it, how these teams come together and how they operate in the larger environment of work and society. The change management specialist is therefore involved in a wide range of activities, often stemming from a particular approach to how individuals work within organizations. This specialist will often come armed with a background in psychology or social science, backed by experience in the working environment at a high level. The idea of change agents – people who can enable change in organizations and who are seen as champions of any change programme – will mean that OD and other change management specialists are most frequently brought in as external consultants.

HRM software design/development

Software designed specifically for HR practitioners has been available for many years. Some deal with particular areas of HRM – recruitment and selection, for example. Others may deal with tracking employee data throughout their employment, from the moment candidates post their CVs, through to the salary grade they achieve, their training programmes, disciplinary record, attendance and absence on holiday or through sickness, and specific bonuses paid. Integrated programs might track the progress of management trainees, checking off their achievement of agreed objectives, the time taken and specific comments from their manager. This might then produce statistics and management reports highlighting how long the trainees take to complete the management programme, how many graduates leave the organization before completing the programme, which educational establishments they came from and what they studied. All these can be incorporated in a single program, or implemented in modular form.

Whether you are involved in selecting and implementing a package, or commissioning a bespoke program as an employee, or designing a new program for a niche-market HRM product as part of a software house, you will need a significant understanding of HRM and the possibilities of its integration and use. For example, an individual's line manager will use the results of a training event at appraisal. Payroll is not the only section that needs to know that an employee has been absent and why. Understanding who should be involved in the selection or commissioning process and significant interviewing and probing skills are required before applying those software planning procedures.

Case Study

Sarbjit is an IT Consultant in the HRM division of a software house.

'I took over a project for this one company: it looked like a complete disaster. The initial work had been done by a salesman who has since left. He basically said that they could have whatever they wanted and made up a price, which had me blinking for a bit out of sheer bewilderment. The company wasn't large but it did have quite a detailed list of requirements that were not exactly run-of-the-mill. There were also quite a few holes in the specification that I couldn't believe they wouldn't want.

I should say here that I was in HRM for a few years, working mainly for a transport company, but I'd always been interested in computers as well and had developed some pretty good packages in my spare time, mainly for the music business, so coming into this job seemed a sensible way of putting the two together. The main area I hadn't really covered was in sales and developing a specification with the client. I'd just designed what I thought would work and interested a few contacts in buying them. The whole business of involving the right people [in preparing the specification] came from my HRM work but of course I suddenly had to become involved in job costing programs and payroll, which I had never touched before.

Anyway, I basically had to go back to the client and start again, pointing out the areas that hadn't been covered in the original specification to the guy who had originally commissioned it. As I got his confidence, I put a proposal to him to carry out the initial exercise again – we would have had to anyway if we weren't going to spend the next year sorting out the problems. As I began to find out what they wanted, I actually found out that they hadn't involved their training department at all! That finally convinced him and I met each of the key managers and a sample of HRM staff as well. The managers who had been involved before were really difficult at first – they wanted to know why they were having to spend more of their time on the same thing. Anyway, most of them came round, when I could point out the advantages – you know, that from what they had specified, we could build a small report program that they could look up any time, that sort of thing. Although, one refused to come round. It turned out that she had given the most detailed information of anyone and had worked quite hard at it the first time. Actually, it really was good and I could see why she didn't want to spend a lot more of her time, so once I had got all the other information, I just checked that she didn't want any of the bells and whistles I could think up – which she didn't – and that was that.

It was a long time in development and luckily they had allocated sufficient of the training budget to cover not just the installation and initial user training but retraining as well. I'm really proud of this one – not only had we developed a pretty good program that we could go to other companies with in their line of work, they even recommended some.'

Summary

In the course of this chapter, the general functions encompassed by HRM have been explained and some of the different skills and requirements from the individual HR professional have been explored. It has been the intention to show that different branches of HRM require slightly different skills and that specialists in any area may become so because these play to their own strengths and abilities and that this reflects their own preferences for working, whether in analysis, communication, development, negotiation or legislation. However, the integration of all these areas of HRM and the ability to use a wide range of skills in different situations will also appeal to the generalist. As a result, HRM has an appeal to a wide range of people from different backgrounds, with no standard educational demands required.

There are, however, some basic similarities. A successful career in HRM demands strong analytical skills, good communication and powers of persuasion, tact and discretion, and an ability to understand a range of activities, not just within HRM but also in other organizational functions. It requires a clear understanding of how to carry out the role as a representative of the organization and a profession, while being seen to be fair even in the more difficult tasks that form a part of HRM. It is not always easy when devising a programme of redundancy, carrying out interviews with staff who are leaving, advising on the terms available when an office or manufacturing plant is relocating to another country or limiting pay increases as a result of reduced profitability or government policy. It used to be said that a good personnel practitioner would always keep a box of tissues to hand. With line managers rather than HR professionals more often breaking such bad news to employees, you might still be tempted to keep them around for personal use. HRM demands personal strength in order to gain the enjoyment of such a wide portfolio of activity and responsibility.

Beyond even the specialist roles outlined here, there are other professions and roles that will use HRM skills or knowledge but indirectly, not as day-to-day practitioners. Despite this, a similar approach is often required, showing the same enthusiasm for the extraordinary variations of behaviour that people in a working environment display.

4 Allied careers

Classically, organizations have developed functions and departments as they grew and were required. A small manufacturing operation may grow and, in order to maintain its competitive edge, need more than one person's insights and therefore calls in additional expertise. Those people gain information from the company's marketing department and become involved in developing and testing new products in the light of that information. They design production tools and the cost of the new product is calculated against an understanding of what the market will bear: the research and development department comes into being. As an organization grows, the HRM department will too, as might a training department, either separately or integrated into the HRM function. However, it is not always necessary to maintain the cost of developing and retaining expertise in certain functions and, as with credit control, specialist organizations have begun to appear which focus solely on carrying out those functions for other organizations. Many organizations have contracted out their payroll function in the same way.

Over the years, there has been a reconsideration of the role of HRM and particularly an emphasis on the impact it can have on organizational strategy. As a result, senior HRM managers and directors have been seen as central to the development of the organization's goals through the best utilization of its employees, rather than as managers of the employment relationship, contracts and statistics. A part of the HRM function has always remained so and has continued to be carried out by HR officers and administrators. With this division in roles, some organizations have seen what they believe is an opportunity to cut costs and retain a reliable source of expertise without the additional burden of employing, training and motivating HR staff. Companies have therefore set themselves up specifically to supply all the administrative functions associated with HRM to other organizations. The original organization can then concentrate on strategy alone, with payroll, attendance figures, training records and many other administrative functions processed externally. These senior HR managers can then gain monthly reports and specially requested information without having to manage it, thereby freeing them to continue in their central role: that of contributing to the organization's success through HR strategy.

This approach, the outsourcing of HRM, is becoming more prevalent in local government and some larger businesses. In some organizations this is carried through to the provision of more complex HRM interventions, such as management or organizational development. Often an organization stuck in the same way of doing things will need an outsider to make recommendations and help carry them out. Smaller organizations adopt this approach as well, when they know they need to change but do not know how. They can also outsource mainstream HR functions that they require in specific situations, for example legal advice on changing contract terms in the light of new legislation.

Case Study

John is a Senior Personnel Manager for a finance company.

'Our relationship with the personnel administration function has always been troublesome. Whether I needed absentee figures broken down by department and function or comparative information on our graduate trainee programme for the last five years, they would always come back with partial data – either they had not checked that information was missing – absence claim forms, for example – or they had not set up a system for collecting the information. So, they would sit someone down with a mound of paper records, which would mean they were not doing their original job and something else would be late, and they would have to sift through it and cobble some figures together. By the time I got it, it was invariably too late. In any case, I still wouldn't ever be sure that the figures were in any way reliable.

I suppose it is because of the sort of company we are but the whole operation is cost-centred [where each department 'charges' another department for any service as if they were completely separate companies]. So, I was completely aware of how much this lack of information was costing me. After seeing an article on that council that hived off the whole of its personnel department, I began to think "Why not here?" So, I researched a bit – it is quite extraordinary how many companies there are out there who do this sort of thing, some blue-chip companies, too. Then I put a tender document together. When you actually sit down and work out all of the different things a personnel department does and then what you really want from them, you have to give them some credit, I suppose.

Of course, I invited the current admin department to tender as well. It is amazing how much they improved over that time. Julie [the personnel administration manager] really got them to knuckle down and concentrate on us, the customers. Two other companies also bid and one of them came in well under budget. It was significantly lower even than the in-house bid. Even with the additional redundancy costs, it looked attractive after a relatively short time, so that was that. With the notice periods of some of the key staff in the old department, there was a reasonable hand-over as well. To date, it's been one of my best decisions – they know they have got to come up with the goods, otherwise, come contract review time, there will be other companies knocking on our door.'

Consultancy

Apart from buying in the HRM administrative function on a contract basis, specialist skills and knowledge can be sourced from consultancies, as discussed in the previous chapter. Some focus on one particular area of HRM. Recruitment and selection agencies in their various guises, from simple research-and-sift organizations through to executive search consultants – headhunters – abound, as well as so-called 'outplacement consultants'. These may be contracted by organizations that are dismissing a significant part of their workforce. These consultants can arrange for career counselling, retraining in new skills, development of CVs and interview skills and, where appropriate, attempt to place those employees who are about to be made redundant in jobs in comparable organizations.

Training and development companies and consultancies are equally varied. Some will concentrate on specific functions – sales, for example – and offer courses in telephone skills for telesales staff, 'closing' techniques for field sales executives or negotiation skills for account managers. Others will offer a range of personal skills training appropriate for a range of employees: active listening, time management or assertiveness. Yet others will concentrate on offering a range of services, from identifying training needs in the organization to evaluating the effectiveness of training or assisting an organization to prepare for accreditation as an Investor in People (IIP). This is a government-sponsored standard that sets a requirement for all training and development opportunities to be evaluated and be linked to the business plan of the organization. These functions may also be carried out in conjunction with Training and Enterprise Councils (TECs) or allied Business Links. Their aim is to stimulate local growth by assisting organizations to become more effective and competitive through the development of the individuals in the organization. They may be involved in general business consultancy or in government initiatives such as IIP, developing Modern Apprenticeships or helping in the assessment of National/Scottish and other Vocational Qualifications.

The Law

A specialization in employment law will not, by its nature, develop from initial involvement in HRM. The route will be legal training and a background in business law, eventually concentrating on aspects of employment or industrial law, either as a solicitor or a barrister. It is also becoming less common for organizations to employ someone in this field directly, requiring a jack-of-all-trades to advise on all matters legal. They will either seek specific advice or retain a lawyer, practice or chambers, for legal opinion or representation. This may concern the implementation and review of employment terms and conditions, the sale of a division or business and the provisions for its employees in redundancy or representation at industrial tribunals. In international terms they will need to deal with differences in employment law in countries across the world and the rights of expatriate employees returning to their 'home' countries. With commerce and the work of even small organizations becoming increasingly international, foreseeing the problems of imposing terms of employment that are unenforceable or that are contrary to the cultural understandings of different countries will become increasingly important. Legal practitioners may also choose to work as a part of an industrial tribunal or appeals panel, hearing and adjudicating on cases between employers and employees.

Academia

Many business schools, either as a part of a university or as private institutions, teach HRM and, often separately, Human Resource Development (HRD). This may be as a part of a course at HND or BTEC level, for a business degree, postgraduate Diploma or Masters level degree. For some modular business degree courses it is possible to take a pathway that emphasizes aspects of HRM. At postgraduate level, there may be specially designed courses in HRM, which integrate general business management skills with the practical and theoretical knowledge necessary to carry out such a job professionally. These will often be linked to gaining membership of the Chartered Institute of Personnel and Development (CIPD) as one of the benefits in taking the course. As a result of this, different learning institutions may offer a wide range of further, specialist modules, such as managing learning processes, international personnel and development or equality management.

Lecturers will be involved in setting the framework for courses, relating them to awards standards set as a part of the charter of the institution or the qualification to be awarded. They will design courses from these outlines, reflecting their own perspectives of the subject, current theory and practice and the learning approaches used in the institution. Delivering the courses may take the form of set lectures in large lecture halls. Alternatively, it might consist of leading seminars, facilitating students' seminars or individual tuition, assisting a student with a management project or research methods. Assessing students' performance through written work, examinations or presentations means that lecturers will have to develop a keen understanding of how performance is assessed. As a result of a series of marking processes, they will have to be able to justify their decisions.

Lecturers are also expected to carry out their own research into current theory and practice in their field. This may then lead to publication in journals, establishing their academic credentials with the possibility of this leading to senior lectureship, with additional responsibilities for academic policy-making. Of course, the career path may lead to a professorship, which will normally require significant published research and could develop an additional career as an author. Many of the current management gurus, treading the lucrative conference circuit and selling books at airports around the world proposing 'fast ways to the top' began with careers in business schools.

Case Study

Judi is a Lecturer in HRD at a university.

'I sort of slowly developed into training. Originally I was working as a senior administrator for a smallish firm – about 250 – and a small part of my job was induction, particular skills training – word-processing packages, that sort of thing – and we had a problem with some of our field technicians. They were the ones in front of the customer but we had different reports about how they behaved when they were actually at the customer's premises. I'd been on a course myself about 'facing the customer' and thought I could revamp it, tailoring it to our operation and the sort of experiences our technicians had to deal with. Now I look back on it, it must have been pretty awful but it did seem to have an effect and I got a real buzz out of it. Probably as a result of that and the fact that the company was growing, I was asked to take on training in the company – researching training providers and courses, arranging for staff to attend and a bit of monitoring. The more I got into it, the more I realized I didn't really know, so I asked to go to university in the evening to study for the Dip. HRD. I'd studied English and philosophy for my BA, so it was easier to get onto a postgrad. course. I even managed to get the firm to sponsor me.

Two years and a lot of hard work later, I was standing there in a gown and funny hat, receiving my award and the Dean asked me on stage what I wanted to do. I just blurted out that I was going on to do my Masters. It was only really then that I think I realized what I wanted to do. In the meantime, I had changed jobs and got into a training company as an administrator – scheduling and organizing training sessions, making sure that we had experienced trainers in whatever subject, that sort of thing. Partly as a result of my pushing – I think I argued that my course needed me to do it – I angled my way into helping develop some sessions and, bit by bit, I started to present parts of the training. Just like before, I really found that I got so much out of being in front of people, having to think on my feet.

With my MA, though, I also got really involved in my research subject – strategy and HRD – and I thought that I could combine the two things I really enjoyed: delivering the lecture and carrying on with the research. So, I asked if I could do some part-time teaching at my university. Now that was scary! Getting to know my way around how the system worked and developing a whole course, and then bending my mind around marking, it all had to be picked up in next to no time. Well, something must have clicked, as I'm now here at [this university] as a full-time lecturer and I'm not sure what I have let myself in for but I've just started my PhD.'

Although it might seem removed from being actively involved in HRM, many lecturers come from a background as a practitioner, or continue to work in HRM but also bring their practical expertise into the institution as a part-time lecturer. In order to teach HRM at a business school, you will normally have to have studied to at least the same level as you teach and have specialist knowledge of HRM. Many institutions are keen to have lecturers with a mix of academic and practical experience, including keen analytical skills. Again, to stand in front of a hall full of students, you have to be something of a performer.

5 Getting started

Top Tips for getting into HRM

Personal development

- Keep up to date with current affairs.
- Read the business pages in the newspapers and financial press.
- Expand your IT skills.
- Consider the key areas of HRM: which interest you most, and why?
- List your key skills and then try to match them against the job descriptions for positions that appeal to you.

Career planning

- Consider the sort of organization that best fits your ways of working and check that the organization you apply to fits this.
- Think whether you can sidestep your way into HRM from a different job within the organization.
- Bring informal experience into an application or interview.
- Do you bring an international dimension to the job – language skills, or having lived in different countries?
- Do you have a different cultural perspective or experience to bring to an organization?
- Accept the need for training and personal development – will the organization offer you a position if you agree to study further?

Your current situation

School/college

First consider what you are doing now. If you are still at school, you should think about what you are good at and how this fits with the various options HRM offers. If you are good at debates or presenting to the class and you can prepare projects using a wide range of materials, you might consider training and development as an option. Similarly, if you are thinking of a career in teaching, this is another allied option. Recruitment and selection will also require good communication and analytic skills but in a different way. Perhaps you are a class representative, perhaps you are interested in subjects that examine how society works, how people behave with one another.

Apart from this, you will have to consider what sort of subjects to study. Of course you will need to be able to communicate well and understand the context of the organization, so language and maths skills will be necessary. Beyond this, although pure science subjects are certainly no bar to becoming an HR professional, an interest in these is likely to steer you in a different direction. Additional languages, social sciences and the humanities are likely to give a breadth of knowledge in preparation for the variety of activities that are carried out in HRM.

Consider what possibilities you might have for job placements. Try to find out about placements within HRM itself. See if temporary holiday jobs offer opportunities for checking how HRM or training and development work. You will be able to gain an understanding of the breadth of activity such departments cover and also gain administrative skills that will help when you are looking for work after school. If you try for a position in HRM, it will be difficult to get in straight from school and you are likely to be confined to an administrative role initially. You will be competing with others who have studied more or have other experience and who are also trying to get into the profession. Ideally therefore you should choose what you study at school and college with an eye to what you will carry on studying in further or higher education.

College/university

If you are at college or university, what are you studying? As with the choices made at school, entry into HRM is more likely to be with a social sciences, humanities or business studies background. Work experience will also count strongly in the selection process and so a degree in biochemistry will not rule you out. A focus on business administration and management information systems may give the basis for a career in a specialized area of HRM. A degree in psychology may open a career path into many branches of the profession, from working in assessment centres to management development. It certainly will not limit you to those areas.

Try to select holiday or part-time jobs as much as is possible to gain direct experience of aspects of HRM. This is still likely to be at an administrative level but may offer the possibility of becoming involved in specific initiatives helping in collating material for a programme of job analysis, or researching the training needs in the organization. Think also of how you can use any course projects to further your involvement in an organization's HR department – how you can relate them to the employment relationship in some way. Talk to your tutor or lecturers in HRM or HRD in the business school. If the course is modular, see if there are particular pathways or modules that you can choose that focus on employment studies or training and development.

HRM, as with many professions, can involve the newly qualified person in that Catch 22: without experience you can't get in but, without the job, you can't gain the experience to get in anyway. Additional experience gained at college or university will help. However, further study at a postgraduate level, perhaps leading to membership of the Chartered Institute of Personnel and Development (CIPD), will give you a distinct advantage and this will be addressed in the following chapter in more detail.

In work/returning to work

If you are in work but looking to change careers, much of what has been stated will still apply. You will benefit from relevant or

Getting started

related qualifications and experience showing that you have the skills required for the particular area of HRM you would most enjoy. If you are experienced in managing employees' performance, you will have been putting many of the required skills into practice. You will also be likely to have worked at some time with the HR department and understand its operation and, in some organizations, its limitations! You might consider secondment to the department or devise a project that draws you into working at a significant level with the HR department. With this it may be possible to be considered for a generalist position in a different organization. Again, you will be competing with people who have operated as HR generalists or who have specific qualifications. Think about enrolling for a part-time course in HRM or HRD alongside your work. This will involve not just a focus on HRM or HRD but also general management knowledge and skills, such as marketing, an understanding of the economic environment, management information systems and organizational behaviour. This should in any case help you develop your own management skills in your current situation.

Case Study

Reece *is a part-time Administration and Personnel Officer and student.*

'I studied music originally and carried on with that for some time. It was poverty, really, that made me decide that I had to go into a more mainstream job. Of course, not many places look on a degree in music as the ideal business qualification and I began to hunt around for retraining opportunities. Accountancy, sales or production just weren't for me and the HRM course at my local university seemed to cover a wide range of business skills. The funding was a bit more difficult, as I'd already done a first degree, but I found out about an obscure foundation that would give grants to people in my situation and the university agreed to my paying in instalments. The placements office found a small firm that was willing, well, begging really, to take a student who would carry out a research project for them. In the end my management report looked at the possibility of introducing an appraisal system into the company and came up with recommendations on how to set it up. They actually carried that out and asked me if I could look at the training aspects of it as well. From that they ended up offering me a part-time job.

Once I had organized the change at university from being a full-time to a part-time student, I was able to start there and I have now completed a full training needs survey for them. The funny thing is that, the more I do, the more they realize needs to be done. So I see the job continuing for some time yet.'

For those who are returning to work, you should consider your skills and abilities in the same way as those who are thinking of changing careers. What have been your experiences, how have you dealt with them and what skills did you need to do so, not just in your past work but in the rest of your life? Think also of any additional skills you have had to use or develop, for example in any voluntary activities you have undertaken. If you had a spell as volunteer coordinator for a local charity, consider what you had to do. In most instances, this will involve recruitment and selection, the organization of activities and the assessment of individuals' capacity to carry them out. It will also demand encouragement and motivation, maybe even discipline – all those things, in fact, that form a part of the line manager's responsibilities for HRM – but without the pay.

Think also of the possibility of retraining at college or university. Vocational courses in HRM and HRD will take into account your working experience as well as your past qualifications. Always enquire about the possibility of gaining a place at college or university rather than believing that your past qualifications were in the wrong subject or were not good enough. You may also qualify for a subsidy or loan, depending on local and national arrangements and the learning institution can help you to determine this as well. On gaining a place to study, think also of organizations you could approach for assistance. Most courses will require projects that are carried out 'live' in an organization. Successfully negotiated projects that have been taken up by the management of the organization in which students have carried out their research have been known to lead to job offers.

Where to look

Qualifications

Again, this may depend on your current situation and on whether you are considering specializing in your current studies or furthering them. In some situations you may be eligible for grants or loans, for example when applying for full-time further or higher education courses for the first time. Bursaries may also be available in particular institutions, for groups of individuals or by competition. This is why it is important to research as much as possible the opportunities open to you, including geographical considerations. Your personal circumstances might constrain you to local choices. Nevertheless, within reach of most people with reasonable access to towns or cities there are usually several institutions from which you may choose. Each will have different approaches to the subjects on offer and some will specialize, for example in international HRM or research in small- and medium-sized enterprises. If you wish to focus on such aspects of HRM, you may have to consider widening your geographical horizons – not every college or university will offer the particular course you are seeking.

You should also think of the supposed reputation of the learning centres you are considering, which, despite evidence to the contrary, is still used by many employers in their selection process. If you believe in the validity of ranked lists saying how good an institution is, there are now many to choose from. *The Times*, amongst others, publishes an annual list, which looks at the performance of departments in universities from an understandable perspective. Universities and colleges will often have details of such ranking on their Web sites, although of course they are going to publish only the information that portrays them favourably. Write to all the business schools or departments that you include in your first choice asking for a prospectus and any details on the courses available in HRM and HRD. Ask for other details too, such as when the course is taught, how much individual time is given to students and how the course is assessed. You may be someone who, given time and support, performs well in written course work but is always pulled down in exams. Some modules in courses are assessed principally by examination. Other institutions assess mainly through course work, which, if you always do well in exams, may not be the best choice.

What your own goals are will also form an important part of your final selection. Why are you considering studying? After all, it is a significant commitment from you in time and maybe money. If you are currently working in HRM, your ultimate goal may be to gain a recognized academic qualification in order to broaden your employment options, to make yourself more attractive in the labour market. On the other hand, if you are considering moving into HRM, or concentrating on it full-time, maybe you need experience of the practical skills necessary to becoming an HR professional. In this case you should seek a course that focuses on that, with a significant component of work or research in a business, charity or the public sector. This may seem a barrier, if you are not working at the moment. However, the college or university will normally assist you in gaining access to an organization, which affords you real experience that will benefit you when you apply for a position in HRM later. You should seek answers to the arrangements available in your chosen short list of institutions.

Although membership of the Chartered Institute of Personnel and Development, or studying for it, is not always demanded from candidates for positions in HRM, it is becoming increasingly common. CIPD membership is currently around 100,000 and employers therefore have a large pool of candidates who are members from which to choose. Given such competition, employers often use membership as a way of distinguishing candidates committed to the profession. So, people often study with the principal aim of gaining the qualifications that give them this 'badge'. In this case, the learning centre should be able to provide a clear link with the CIPD's published professional standards.

Distance learning is another option, where it would be impossible to attend a college or university full-time. This is sometimes seen as less preferable, with doubts about the quality of the course or its acceptability to potential employers. In fact, some of the distance learning options available can be the most challenging and highly regarded of qualifications available. Checking that the

Getting started

course on offer is fully accredited by a reputable educational establishment (normally a university or the CIPD for private learning organizations) should be an additional question put to the institution offering it. Employers also favourably consider qualifications gained through distance learning from reputable institutions. The ability to study as a self-guided and disciplined individual is most often seen as a strength in a candidate.

Probably the most famous of distance-learning opportunities is offered by the Open University, with home-based learning tools, including learning packs and the famous television 'lectures', supplemented by pre-arranged contact with personal tutors and occasional weekend residential courses, together with a summer school. However, the Open University is by no means the only learning centre to offer distance learning, with many other colleges, universities and other institutions such as the CIPD and private training colleges providing guided courses ranging from the academic to the highly practical. A word of warning here: distance learning offers a structured, often well-supported way of developing your skills and furthering your qualifications without having to attend an institution frequently. However, its success depends on the sort of person you are. Think whether you are good at organizing yourself, sitting down and studying when other opportunities seem more appealing. Consider whether you can arrange your life at home to gain the peace and quiet you will need. Do you have the resources to carry out the assignments, for example access to a reasonable library, in addition to what the college or university will provide? If you can answer yes to these questions, then distance learning may provide an ideal way to further your career aspirations while dealing with all your other responsibilities. It may also be cheaper.

Applying for courses

If you are applying for a first degree or HND course, this is dealt with centrally by the Universities and Colleges Admission Service (UCAS) in the UK or the Central Applications Office in Galway for the Republic of Ireland. The UCAS Web site – www.ucas.ac.uk – has a list of courses, the places where they can be studied and a list of the basic entry requirements, for example A levels or leaving certificates. More information can be gained from the UCAS guidebook, which should be available from your school or local careers service.

Once you have researched the best courses at the available learning institutions (you should apply directly to private colleges), you can apply to several institutions, placing them in order of preference. Careers advisory services will help you in this. You apply a year in advance of the academic year you wish to start the course. You may then be offered an unconditional acceptance from one or any of your choices. This means that you should complete your current studies and be available for the course for the academic year you made your application. You may also be offered a place conditional on your achieving certain qualifications, for example two grade Bs at A level. If you do not achieve this for your first choice but it is sufficient for your second choice, this is the university or college at which you should start your course. Some universities might hold an open day, or invite you to interview before offering you a place.

If you are applying for a higher degree – a postgraduate certificate, diploma or masters degree – or for a part-time course, even if it is a first degree, you must apply directly to the university or college. Enquire from the particular institution what their application procedure is and particularly by when you need to apply. If it is a first application, you may still gain financial assistance.

Finance

You will have to find money for two things while studying: tuition fees and your living costs. If you are applying for the first time for a higher education degree then you may have help with the tuition fees, which is administered by your Local Education Authority. Similarly loans are available to help with living costs. You should contact your Local Education Authority for an application form. The loan must be repaid after you have completed your course, you have returned to work and are earning above a specified amount. The sums are not huge and realistically many students have to add to the income from the loan by any part-time work they can find. For grants in the Republic of Ireland, you should contact the Higher Education Grants Section of your local authority. General information can be gained from the Higher Education Grants Section of the Department of Education and Science.

In some circumstances it is possible to gain additional support. If you are a mature student, have dependants, are a single parent or are disabled, you should be able to gain additional funding that you do not have to repay. The university or college may also have specific bursaries that you may apply for. Most also have a hardship fund from which they might grant additional support for unexpected changes in circumstances. There are also private sources of grants; a useful starting point is The Grants Register.

Jobs

The way you approach looking for jobs will depend on your current circumstances: whether you are in work at the moment, the extent of your relevant experience and your qualifications. Your access to the resources that will help you, from libraries and careers advisory services to ranges of magazines and newspapers as well as the availability of Internet access, will aid you in your search for a job in HRM.

If you are at school or out of work, there is a range of possibilities available to you. Apart from seriously considering the importance of gaining further qualifications, which have already been discussed, you should first consider your own qualities and experience against the examples shown in the case studies. Where there are gaps, think how you can develop yourself or do something to gain the additional experience.

Careers advice is available from many sources. The Employment Service, often through jobcentres, will have dedicated careers advisers, who can advise on the relevance of your skills, qualifications and experience to a career in HRM. They will be likely to have links with local colleges, universities, trainers and employers. As an employment service, they will also have a range of jobs being advertised, some of which may be in a related field, for which they may have job descriptions. These will help to broaden your understanding of the range of activities carried out in the field of HRM. If you have completed a degree, or are in the process of doing so, you can also seek advice from the Association of Graduate Careers Advisory Services (AGCAS). Your best starting point is your current or past college or university. There are also some private careers advisers that advertise in local and specialist papers and magazines, some of which offer a professional service. As with choosing a college or university, it is important that you check the quality of the service on offer and compare the prices charged for their services. Some will do little more than rewrite your curriculum vitae; others will give a complete service, advising on additional skill requirements and how best to gain them, as well as alternative approaches to gaining a foothold in HRM.

Without some direct experience of working in HRM, you are likely to have to demonstrate the relevance of your past activity and knowledge in order to gain a position. Voluntary work can be a very useful way of building this up. Many not-for-profit and other types of organization will employ HR professionals who may use volunteers with general skills that are appropriate to working in HRM. You will still have to prove your suitability. However, gaining a placement as a volunteer should be simpler than trying for a paid position. As a volunteer in such an organization, you will be able to gain a useful overview of the function of HRM as well as developing useful experience, referees and contacts. Use these and other contacts to increase your employability in the field. You are unlikely to be offered a job in HRM simply by knowing an HR professional but you can contact them suggesting your availability to assist with projects in the department on a voluntary basis.

Despite the range of assistance the Employment Service can offer, it is unlikely that many dedicated or senior positions in HRM will be advertised through jobcentres. They are most frequently advertised in the local, national and international press as well as specialist magazines, such as *People Management* and increasingly on the Internet. Local newspapers are a good source of entry-level positions in HRM and HRD and sometimes more senior jobs as well. Training and development organizations and those with dedicated training and development departments, while often demanding graduates in fields related to the training delivered, will also consider applicants with relevant experience. A psychology graduate who has specialized in the process of learning and an IT practitioner with experience of training others in his or her organization may both be considered for positions in a commercial training organization.

National newspapers will specialize on certain days in HRM vacancies, although often among other general managerial and professional positions. Vacancies in the national press will frequently also advertise in a separate section for senior managerial and director-level appointments in HRM. *The Telegraph* on Thursdays and *The Guardian* on most days, depending on the sector, are useful starting points. The latter also posts these vacancies on its Web site: www.jobsunlimited.co.uk. Many other Internet sites acting as virtual recruitment agencies spring up daily. The financial and international press will often advertise senior HRM positions that involve either working abroad as a part of the job or as a resident of another country. Some positions advertised in the national and international press for a multinational organization will require a significant amount of mobility, acting as an integrator of policy worldwide or as an international troubleshooter.

Case Study

Morgan is an HR Advisor in Group Culture in an international health care product manufacturer and distributor.

'Although I enjoyed my degree in psychology, I wasn't really sure about what I wanted to do with it. I just fell into studying it, without fitting it into any idea of a career. So after university I drifted a bit in administrative jobs, eventually moving into a training organization as administrator and slowly edged my way into training itself – the classic route. As a part of the deal, I had to study further, become a member of the CIPD and get my Dip.HRM [postgraduate diploma]. So there I was, studying again – and enjoying it. Despite the fact that I was in training, I decided to keep my options open and chose the HRM pathway, rather than concentrating on HRD, although I broadened this out by choosing modules in strategic HRM and HRD, managing change, management development and so on. I thought I might as well carry on and do the MA and I concentrated on management development and cultural difference.

Partly as a reward for getting my MA and partly because [the training organization] was moving much more into management development, I started to spend more of my time on this, rather than specific skills training. For me it was really challenging, moving from standing and delivering more or less set training courses to management development. Sitting with a group of managers, coaching, rather than delivering, having a framework and a set of tools but no absolute destination – that's what was so fascinating: sort of giving them a kick-start and seeing where it would lead.

It was a particular group of managers from [a multinational biosciences company] – and some of them had been seconded from Switzerland, some from the [United] States – that really brought me back to my MA. They were having huge difficulties in their approaches to development – that individual versus group thing, where some were demanding the most attention for their personal projects at the expense of others. Some would sit there seething and saying nothing. Others would object strongly, saying that the individualist had completely misunderstood the point of the session. So I suggested we look at cultural approaches to management and development as a central theme of the programme, which began to break down the antagonism.

Then I saw the advert for this job in the *Financial Times*. It was quite a selection process: initial interview, assessment centre and a weekend residential assessment. I felt like I'd been through the mill but it certainly makes you feel you'd want to be a part of the company, which I am. Apart from that, I'd studied and then gone straight into work: there wasn't the money to take a year out or anything like that. So, I felt that, apart from continuing something that had become a theme in my working life, I could finally begin to see more of the world – I certainly do that!'

Whether you are thinking of moving into a career in HRM or expanding your work in a related field, whether you are at school, college, in or out of work, there are many approaches you can take. In the end, you are likely to have to undertake further study at some point in order to enter a profession that, like other professions, demands a constant review of your skills and knowledge and your abilities in relating them to the organization. Being an HR professional requires a commitment to your own development, seeing opportunities and planning your future capabilities – your career. In this chapter, you will have seen many options to help you in this, whatever your current situation. In the next, you can investigate the variety of qualifications that may form a part of your own development plan.

Your personal development plan

- **Where am I now?** Draw up a list of the skills you have had to use in the past and the experience you have gained (whether paid or not).
- **What am I good at?** List the knowledge and skills that have helped you to achieve the things you want and think of how you applied them.
- **What interests me about HRM?** Consider each of the elements of HRM in turn – each of the subjects in chapter 3 – and the skills, knowledge and abilities required for each. Which areas interest you? Look at advertisements for HRM and define why some jobs interest you and others do not.
- **Match yourself with your interests.** Where do your own skills, knowledge and abilities match those of the elements of HRM outlined? Where do they not match? What do your chosen job advertisements require that you do not have?
- **What can't I do?** Consider the skills, knowledge and abilities that you need to develop as a result. Think about the tips in this chapter and discount any options that will not help you or are definitely not open to you.
- **So what do I do?** Research the remaining options thoroughly, using the suggestions here and from the useful addresses and further reading at the back of this book. Think of the time and money you may require but above all think of which option will be the most stimulating and enjoyable.
- **Plan your campaign.** Once you have chosen the best approach for you, plan how you are going to carry it out. Be prepared to change your plan when circumstances change.
- **Finally** – Do it!

6 Qualifications

The requirement for qualifications or experience

The age-old problem of experience versus qualifications in gaining a job, or in progressing in your career, is no different in HRM. It is possible to gain certain positions with experience equivalent to that gained in a practically based qualification. Typically, this will be at administrator or senior managerial level. Intervening levels will more often demand either the possession of a relevant qualification or a signal of your willingness to work for one (maybe evidence that you are already enrolled on a course). At its most basic, administration in HRM involves standard office skills, such as a basic knowledge of word-processing, spreadsheet and database use and input. You will need to type accurately at a reasonable speed, the ability to take on projects and work to set deadlines, work on your own initiative and be able to contribute to teamwork. Qualifications in such administrative skills, for example from the RSA Examination Board, will therefore be an advantage.

However, not all administration jobs are confined to basic office skills. Especially if you are assisting in a particular aspect of HRM, for example in a training needs analysis or a recruitment and selection programme, past experience in matching raw data against set criteria may be significant, even though it has not been in the field of HRM. At a senior level, certain organizations may require a high level of knowledge of an aspect of the business or operations of the organization that is not usually a part of the HR professional's remit. As a result of an increased involvement by line managers in the activities of HRM – recruitment and selection, performance appraisal, identifying training needs – a senior manager from a different function may be appointed as the head or a part of a team to lead a particular HRM project. This is particularly likely of an operational manager or director heading HRM as a part of her or his remit to effect significant change in the organization.

Relevant experience may therefore be more appropriate than specific HRM qualifications in certain instances. Nevertheless, it is clear from looking through job advertisements that most would at least prefer, if not demand, a qualification in HRM. Note also how often they add those weasel words 'or equivalent experience'. Never avoid applying for a job where it says that something is only desirable. There are, however, a large number of qualified or part-qualified people around who could, in theory, be competing for that position. Of course, many have other interests than those you are pursuing, others are seeking jobs at a different level and some are working in allied professions rather than directly in HRM. Others still will not be looking to change their jobs. This still leaves quite a few who are looking and have a piece of paper that states that, at least once, some time ago, they made a commitment to understanding the practice of HRM. As most employers will look on this favourably as a part of the candidate's application, your equivalent experience without a qualification is going to have to be quite special. Add to this the likelihood of your having to gain a qualification during your career in HRM and it may pay for you to consider starting early.

Although it is frequently possible to study HRM in its own right, both theoretically and practically, many courses are designed to lead to acceptance as a graduate member of the Chartered Institute of Personnel and Development (CIPD). This, rather than a specific qualification, is most frequently stated as an application requirement for a job in HRM. Despite this, if you have an equivalent qualification that has not automatically led to membership of the CIPD, you should not be put off applying. It is often possible to consider elements of your qualification and experience as exempting you from parts of the qualification route to CIPD membership and these will be examined later in this chapter.

The advantages of gaining a qualification that links to CIPD membership seem clear when considering the possible competition from existing members for the jobs you may seek to gain. There are many other benefits of becoming a member. For an annual fee, some of the major tangible benefits can be summarized as access to a significant, specialized library, a free legal advisory service and a free copy of the fortnightly magazine, *People Management*, which is a major source of advertised HRM vacancies. Additionally, the CIPD has a network of local branches, which provides an opportunity to meet other HR professionals, gaining support and advice, as well as regular forums and lectures on contemporary subjects. These can range from developments in managing reward to updates on the latest employment legislation. Information on other services, including detailed information on the routes to membership and available qualifications can be obtained from the CIPD itself.

In considering an appropriate qualification, you should again assess your current position and the possible routes through to achieving your goals. Do not just think of working in HRM but consider the types of organization you would want to work in, whether you would want to specialize and, if so, in what. If you are still at school, what have you chosen to study, is there an appropriate course locally, maybe an HND in business studies with an HRM option, and how does it lead to gaining the ultimate qualification you require? If you are considering higher education, you may choose a postgraduate diploma from the local university or college but check: does it fit with your child care arrangements and is the focus on industrial relations really going to help you into training and development?

Case Study

Joan is a Personnel Officer for a medium-sized stationery supplier.

'I've actually been here five years now. Originally I thought I was quite lucky to get in. There were quite a lot of candidates for the Personnel Administrator's job I applied for. Anyway, I was quite happy for a while, getting to know all the different jobs that were necessary: preparing the statistics for equal opportunities, scheduling and collating appraisals, updating personnel records.

After about a year, I began to get itchy – you know, for getting involved in more interesting work, more unpredictable things, but that was [the previous Personnel Officer's] job. I didn't really see how I could move on as she was always blocking any moves I made to get more involved. Anyway, she suddenly left and instead of giving me the opportunity, they recruited someone from outside [the organization]. To be honest, she was pretty clueless, but it did mean that I could start picking up new jobs and really doing things that mattered. When she left as well, I pointed out to her boss what I had been doing and was interviewed with the other external candidates. I suppose I could show that I could do the job and I got it. Anyway, after that – the same problem. My boss kept saying that I couldn't really go further without CIPD [membership] but wouldn't give me any support to get it. So, I looked at [the local higher education college] for part-time courses that would get me the CIPD [qualification] and it seemed like I would be able to get in with my experience. I was just so excited that I would be accepted that I didn't really look too much at the content of the course. Then I got to thinking – "Why am I doing a course that seems to concentrate so much on the theory at the expense of the practical?" I mean – post-modern perspectives in organizational analysis! I could see that going down well at [the stationery company].

I thought – this place has offered to take me, so others might as well. I looked around some more – the Internet is brilliant for this – and [a college about 90 miles distant] seemed to offer much more the sort of course I wanted and they ran it as a distance learning option. It was much more practically based, although they stressed that I would still be covering the subject from an academic point of view. They could even arrange for me to work in a different organization at weekends, rather than this one, when it came to practical course work. As [my organization] had hardly helped me so far, I thought they wouldn't be likely to start now and allow me working time to research things they weren't interested in.

To be fair to them, I showed them my first year's grades in my appraisal and since then they have agreed that I can have time to work on my agreed projects for the second year, which gives me some weekends free now, at least!'

Routes to qualification

Although it is feasible to study for a qualification in HRM or HRD, which is not linked to gaining CIPD membership, a majority of courses are designed to provide a pathway to this. Therefore, a detailed breakdown of the route to membership of the CIPD is key to understanding your qualification options.

There are essentially three ways of achieving the professional standards required by the CIPD for membership:

- professional education;
- professional assessment against CIPD standards;
- assessment against national standards.

In all cases you will need to apply to join the CIPD before being accepted for the course or assessment.

Professional education

If you wish to gain a professional qualification, you will need to apply to a recognized centre, normally a college or university or alternatively a distance learning option from accredited private institutions. The CIPD retains a full current list of its accredited centres included in its booklet *Qualification Guidelines*, which is also available through its Web site: www.cipd.co.uk.

You may have completed other courses that give you part-exemption from one or more modules of the CIPD professional qualification scheme. This means that suitably accredited courses leading to HNC and HND in business studies, NVQ/SVQ levels 4 and 5 and some degrees in business studies can lead to an award of 'advanced standing'. Therefore you can gain recognition that you have already satisfied the requirements for one or more modules of the CIPD's core management field – one of three fields required for achieving graduate membership. In some instances it may also be possible to consider courses that have not been officially accredited for such an exemption as well. In all cases this should be discussed with the learning institutions you are thinking of attending.

Professional assessment against CIPD standards

If you have relevant professional experience but have no recognized qualifications, then you can apply to an approved professional assessment centre. This option is open to current HRM professionals, who are actively involved in the practice of HRM in their workplace. You should probably have had experience in this role for about five years. As the assessment considers strategic aspects of HRM, you are likely to be working at a managerial level. It is therefore not a route for people with general management experience or with limited specialist experience in one area of HRM. The professional assessment centre will offer advice on how to prepare evidence of your work that proves your ability against the CIPD's professional standards. Where there is no evidence available of a particular element of the assessment you will be able to undertake courses to cover this. For example, if you have been working solely in management development, you might not have evidence of other generalist or managerial skills such as human resource planning or statistical analysis.

Assessment against national standards

This approach is based on assessing your competence in the workplace through particular National Vocational Qualifications (NVQ) or Scottish Vocational Qualifications (SVQ). It is therefore only suitable if you are already in work in an HRM or HRD environment and have some experience of organizational strategy. Again, you will assess your current performance against the requirements of each NVQ/SVQ and develop an action plan in order to build a portfolio of evidence that can be assessed by an accredited centre. The CIPD can provide a full list of centres that are approved for NVQ/SVQs in HRM and HRD. These include the Business and Technology Education Council (BTEC) and the City & Guilds of London Institute (C&G), the Pitman Examination Institute (PEI), the RSA Examinations Board, the Scottish Qualifications Authority and the CIPD itself. Flexible learning courses offered by these centres can cover the required knowledge elements that cannot be demonstrated in the workplace.

The qualifications

Certificate level qualifications

For people with limited experience of studying in HRM or HRD, there are two intermediate qualifications that lead to the award of NVQ/SVQ level 3 and eligibility to become an Associate Member of the CIPD: the Certificate in Personnel Practice (CPP) and the Certificate in Training Practice (CTP). As both course titles suggest, these are strongly based on understanding the approaches and demonstrating the practice of the elements of HRM and HRD. The CPP therefore focuses on projects covering, amongst others, recruitment and selection, designing training events and demonstrating an ability to consider discipline and grievance interviews. You will also have to demonstrate a knowledge of the issues that underpin these practices, such as the relationship of each practice to the organizational context and the significance of codes of conduct and equal opportunities.

As it is practically based, CPP is most appropriate for people in work who are either currently not working directly in the field of HRM or who have just begun. It can therefore be useful to gain a structured approach and a recognized qualification at personnel administrator or officer level. It is also frequently available as a distance or flexible learning package from the usual educational establishments but also quite widely from private training providers. Some will offer a course that starts with a week when the subject and the assignments are introduced, after which you will have a period to carry out the assignments in the workplace and write them up. This structure will then be repeated until all elements of the course have been completed.

This approach is true for the CTP as well. However, this will concentrate on projects such as identifying learning needs, defining learning objectives and instructing learners as well as demonstrating knowledge of the principles of adult learning and of evaluating success against learning outcomes. As a result, CTP is appropriate to those wishing to move into training and development and to those newly involved in it at training administrator or officer level. Both CPP and CTP can be seen as a part of the path to gaining full graduate membership of the CIPD through what they call the Professional Qualification Scheme.

Professional Qualification Scheme

Accredited courses at postgraduate diploma level in colleges and universities may be structured in very different ways and may offer options that you should consider carefully before deciding on the institution at which you want to study. Nevertheless, if they are accredited, they will have to conform to a rationale stipulated by the CIPD that comprises three fields of study:

- core management;
- core personnel and development;
- specialist and generalist personnel and development electives.

For each field you must complete four modules. Having completed one field you are eligible for associate membership of the CIPD. The successful completion of all three fields makes you eligible for graduate membership as well as a recognized postgraduate qualification. As a result of the assessment of prior learning you may be awarded 'advanced standing'. This means that there is flexibility built into achieving each field: core management might be gained through an NVQ/SVQ level 4/5, specialist/generalist personnel and development electives by an assessment of prior learning and core personnel and development through a structured course at a learning institution.

Each module is assessed by assignments, some of which will be work-based, examinations and the preparation of a management report. If you are not in work, the learning institution will often have a placements office. Here, organizations seeking students who are looking for study and work placements can be matched with those students who have no contact with a suitable organization, either because they are not in work or their organizations are uncooperative.

Core management

As HRM is more than a support function within the organization, it is clearly important that general business and management skills will figure strongly in the working life of the HR professional. This field of study therefore concentrates on four modules, which attempt to balance knowledge and understanding of business management on the one hand and the competence to put this into practice on the other:

- managing activities;
- managing in a business context;
- managing people;
- managing information.

The managing activities module concentrates on three areas: the nature of managerial work, the work environment and quality and continuous improvement. Firstly, it examines the fact that managers' working experience is diverse and fast-moving, that it requires establishing priorities through analysis and planning and that it involves working and communicating with other people. This experience must take account of how the organization is structured, the way people do things and the limitations imposed by law on the operation of the organization. Finally, managers must consider what the organization is there for: its users and customers and how to ensure that the employees provide them with an acceptable quality of service or product.

Managing in a business context also considers three key elements: strategy, the factors affecting the organization and the position of the organization in society. This means that you will consider how corporate and HRM strategy are formed. You will also study the fact that organizations must plan in the context of constant changes in the national and international economic, political, social and legal climate as well as changes in technology.

In a managerial role, it is clear that providing information and motivating groups of people demands an understanding of how people work in an organization, how differences in their expectations affect this and the extent to which managers can lead those groups of people to maximize performance. The managing people module therefore considers how the design of the organization and the patterns of behaviour by groups of employees can affect performance. It seeks to understand how power is used in the organization, what relationship it has to leadership and the ethical basis of employing people. Within this context it also questions how individuals are motivated.

Organizations are systems that depend on gaining information and communicating it efficiently. The managing information module therefore examines some of the key functions in an organization, for example accounting and finance in order to understand the link of HRM to profitability and budgeting. It will also consider how to gain marketing statistics and understand how they can contribute to a greater understanding of possible future organizational strategies. Of course, in order to do this, it is necessary to have an understanding of the methods of gaining, storing, analysing and communicating information, including by electronic means, as well as how this information is used to make decisions.

Core personnel and development
As has been seen, many HR professionals may tend to specialize in certain areas of HRM – training and development or recruitment and selection, for example. The core personnel and development field ensures that this experience is understood in the context of the full range of the ways that HRM can affect the success of the organization. It therefore considers all the functions outlined in Chapter 3: gaining diverse employees, their development and reward, how management and employees consult and negotiate and how this is managed, including the use of IT. In order to do this, the modules also cover the context of HRM: what HRM is considered to be and the fact that it is different from organization to organization. They also cover the differing roles of HRM and what it means to be a 'professional' HRM practitioner as well as the fact that HRM does not act in a vacuum but is affected by labour markets and the skills available, laws and trade unions.

Specialist and generalist personnel and development electives
The third field offers a range of options, from which you may choose four modules. Very few organizations will offer all of them

and again this is something you should check when choosing the learning institution you wish to attend. Some will offer a spread of options, others may have a specialist tutor in a particular field, for example reward, which may limit your future career options. In this instance, a desire to move into recruitment and selection or training and development, while not ruled out by choosing such electives, will not prepare you for the depth of knowledge and practice that you will need.

The options are based around the standard areas of competence in HRM:

- employee resourcing;
- employee development;
- employee reward;
- employee relations.

There are two further strategic options available. Each of these areas may have up to six modules from which you can choose. Employee resourcing has up to five: selection and assessment centres, human resource planning, international personnel and development, organizational consultancy and health and safety. Employee development has six possible modules: management development, vocational education and training, managing learning processes, managing training operations, managing technology-based training and the transition and transformation of organizations. Employee reward consists of four possible modules: pensions, performance management, equality management and career management. Employee relations again has four possible choices of module: employment law, international employee relations, employee involvement and communications, and employee counselling, support and welfare. The final two options are strategic HRM/HRD and managing change.

This is a significant and almost bewildering range of options, which most learning institutions will not be able to offer in full. Some, particularly those that offer distance learning, will offer most of these, even if they are not necessarily called exactly the same. As most courses are offered on a reasonably flexible basis, you may not have to choose your electives before you start the course. As a result you may have time to get a feel for the subject and then understand better your preferred specialist subjects. You should also consider carefully whether you wish to concentrate on one of the four major strands – resourcing, development, reward or relations – or whether you would do better to spread your acquisition of skills across the board in order to broaden your generalist skills. This will depend on your current situation, your understanding of the possibilities available to you and your own preferences for particular subjects.

The management report
In addition to the modules in these three fields, you will also have to complete a management report. This will require you to take on the role of consultant in an organization, either your own or a placement organization, and to consider with key people what HRM problems or opportunities could benefit from investigation. As with any consultancy, this should take into account the many facets of the organization – what is affecting it, what its current strategies are and how they fit to your chosen subject. This can be anything from the introduction of HR management software through the identification of training needs to a survey of the communications systems in the organization.

Once the project aims are agreed, you need to design a method for investigating the issue further and carry this out, collecting data from records, by sending out questionnaires or perhaps by interviewing selected individuals in the organization. Analysing your findings, coming up with your conclusions as a result of this and promoting a series of recommendations that are suitable to the organization will all form a part of the final management report.

The qualified HRM professional

Whatever method you take to gain your qualifications, a part of any understanding of being professional is the state of your current knowledge, skills and abilities. Just after qualifying, these are likely to be up-to-date and practised using approaches and techniques that have been recently developed. As a professional, you will want your performance to stay that way and so you will need to regularly review your own performance against new theories, alternative models of working, additional techniques that are available to you. This will form a part of an action plan and performance against this will in turn form a part of your assessment to becoming a full (corporate) member of the CIPD. This process of continuing professional development (CPD) is intended to be a lifelong, planned approach to your own learning. This should therefore equip you not just for your current workplace but for changes in your career or direction in HRM. For example, a decision to move specifically into training and development, or a desire to move from the City's demands into developing a charity, will require a different approach and the use of skills other than the ones you are currently exercising. If developing skills outside your day-to-day needs forms a part of your planned personal development, then these changes can be made as a natural part of your career.

7 The future of human resource management

Given the increasing professional membership of the Chartered Institute of Personnel and Development, there is a continuing and expanding demand for the skills, perceptions and strategic advice that HRM brings to organizations. Whether this indicates an increase in the number of people involved at some level in the practice of HRM, or whether previously unqualified or underqualified practitioners are choosing to study and gain membership is difficult to say. There are still many people working in HRM at all levels of every sort of organization without formal recognition of their professionalism. There is no information available to say that these people are any less proficient than their qualified counterparts. There *is* evidence that, on average, professionals with relevant qualifications are able to command higher reward packages than those without. It can also be seen that many organizations require employees to study and develop existing and new skills while they are working. The CIPD mirrors many other professional bodies in requiring individuals to prepare and implement a programme of continuous professional development.

Many organizations now understand that a glib statement of how their employees are their most important asset is not enough. They have begun to realize that the HRM professional must be involved at every level of the organization, including not just the HR strategy but also the organization's business strategy. As a result, there is a certain parallel with the job profiles found in the United States with more vacancies for personnel or HR directors being advertised. This extends the career path for the HR professional throughout the organization and demands much more of that person, whatever function he or she currently performs. It will no longer be sufficient to be an efficient and knowledgeable generalist within the bounds of our understanding of HRM. Future HR professionals may not even be called that at all. Instead they may be seen as general or specialist business managers, such as operations or logistics managers. They will also happen to have studied and put into practice a range of strategies and actions that are concerned with the deployment of individuals to the best advantage of the organization – business-people managers

Perhaps this will be seen only in some types of organization, with others preferring to retain HR managers and directors with specific responsibilities and expertise derived from a continuing involvement in the cutting edge developments of a specialist subject. Even then, generalist HR professionals are likely to be called upon to know a range of business techniques greater than ever before, from industry-specific processes to an understanding of the effects of a particular HR strategy on the profit and loss accounts of the organization. A part of their CPD will therefore have to consider knowledge usually thought of as the province of other managers: accounting, marketing, even statistical analysis. This may seem increasingly challenging but also draws HRM from a support function into the heart of the operation and direction of the organization.

This move, from employing people with a narrow range of knowledge and skills matched to a particular job to using the much wider abilities that an employee will be called upon to demonstrate, means that the role of the training and development specialist will also change. Already many organizations realize that throwing training indiscriminately at a problem is ineffective and that, in employing a diverse range of people, what they learn and how they learn will demand more individual approaches to training and development. The requirement for any training and development intervention to increase enjoyment, confidence, productivity and profitability and particularly to assist in the change of an organization's culture reflects the necessity for HRM to anticipate the organization's needs rather than to react to requests for particular training programmes. The importance of management and leadership will mean an ever increasing focus on the link of management style and practice to the culture of the organization. No longer will the management development specialist reach for a ready-made solution to a problem but he or she will have to consider the future needs of the organization, what sort of leadership will be required and what will have to be done to gain that. This specialist will therefore have to consider and be a part of the organization's strategy and have a cross-functional knowledge in order to create the best development opportunities.

What of other HR specialists? If the traditional HR functions such as selection and performance appraisal are carried out by line managers, does this mean that the only options in the future will be as an occasional resource when those line managers or business-people managers need advice outside their day-to-day range of experience? If so, then those specialists are unlikely to be employed by one organization but will become a resource to be called upon when needed. They will be employed or self-employed consultants and attached to a company that provides such specialist HR professionals, either concentrating on that specialism or as one of a number of specialist activities.

This approach, what has become known as outsourcing, may apply not just at such senior levels but may also be used for the everyday administrative functions of HRM. Despite a concentration on developing the scope of activities at a strategic level, HRM still relies on many administrative functions, from compiling the results of employee surveys to preparing absence reports. Some organizations will reorganize this administrative function with the help of HR software, which will demand different skills from those currently used to carry out the task. Other organizations are beginning to see a value in focusing on strategic issues and subcontracting the general administration to other companies, which may have invested in dedicated and advanced HR software to give additional analytical clout to management decision-making. Although both of these appear to reduce the need for HR administration employees, this may not necessarily be the case. If more organizations outsource their administration, more companies will need those very skills that have been outsourced. As a result of the availability of more sophisticated analyses of employee data, managers will often require more detailed statistics, tailored to their own organizations. While this will require different skills, particularly those in IT, and a shift to more project-working – the HR administrator is likely to carry out work for several organizations with different deadlines – it may not mean a reduction in the amount of people working in HRM.

The changing nature of work and the way in which organizations look for flexibility from their employees will obviously have a significant impact on the practice of HRM and the skills required of HRM professionals. As long as organizations employ people there will be a need for people with the specialist knowledge and approach of the HR professional. As organizations change as a result of economic necessity or political will, from a greater understanding of their social responsibilities or the nature of competition, so will the organizations' requirements from their employees change and all who work for them in whatever capacity. Just as these workers will have to alter their expectations and skills, so will HR professionals. Of course they will also have to take on board new ways of adopting, adapting and rewarding workers' abilities and the idea of human resource management itself will then have altered, perhaps out of all recognition. Such a varied and variable career may not suit everyone but for those who see the challenge and possibilities in HRM, whatever its complexion in each different organization, there will continue to be a unique experience and a rewarding career.

8 Further information

Where to study

Information on courses and learning institutions in the UK from:

UCAS
Rosehill
New Barn Lane
Cheltenham
Gloucestershire GL52 3LZ

You can also search their Web site for details of courses, learning institutions and application criteria: www.ucas.ac.uk

Applicant enquiries: (01242) 227788
General enquiries: (01242) 222444
Minicom: (01242) 544942 (This service is designed for people with hearing difficulties)
Application pack requests:
Tel: (01242) 223707
E-mail: app.rec@ucas.ac.uk
General applicant enquiries: enq@ucas.ac.uk

Copies of the University and College Entrance Guide are available from Sheed and Ward Ltd whose address is listed over.

Sheed and Ward Ltd
14 Coopers Row
London EC3N 2BH
Tel: (020) 7702 9799
Fax: (020) 7702 3583

Copies of the COSHEP/UCAS Entrance Guide to Higher Education in Scotland are available from:

James Thin Booksellers
53–59 South Bridge
Edinburgh EH1 1YS
Tel: (0131) 556 6743
Fax: (0131) 557 8149

John Smith and Son
57 St Vincent Street
Glasgow G2 5TN
Tel: (0141) 221 7472
Fax: (0141) 248 4412

Sheed and Ward Ltd
14 Coopers Row
London EC3N 2BH
Tel: (020) 7702 9799
Fax: (020) 7702 3583

Try to obtain a copy of the *UCAS Handbook* from your school or local careers office before contacting UCAS.

For courses in the Republic of Ireland, contact the Central Applications Office. Addresses for the four universities are listed in the next chapter. In addition, the twelve technical colleges also offer training and development opportunities in HRM.

The CIPD also lists available courses in the UK and the Republic of Ireland in its booklet, *Qualification Routes*.

The Internet

The Internet is a major source of information for people wanting to consider studying HRM. It may be used to seek possible grant and job opportunities, and to search for universities, colleges and private training organizations that offer the full range of courses in HRM. These may offer significant detail in the range of study options, admission requirements and the subjects that can be combined with HRM.

There are also many opportunities to look for jobs on the Internet. Although many vacancies that are advertised are slanted towards IT professionals, this is becoming much less prevalent. A much wider spread of professional vacancies is available from private recruitment agencies, from dedicated web-based job sites and from offshoots of paper-based newspaper and magazine advertising, for example *The Guardian* Web site: www.jobsunlimited.co.uk.

Access to the web is not limited to private ownership of a computer. Most public libraries now have computing facilities and some offer free access to the Internet. They will normally offer training in accessing the web and how best to use the tools available to gain the information you are seeking. Check your local library network for the terms on which you can use their computers. You normally have to book time in advance and there are usually also limitations on how long you can use them in any one stretch.

Useful publications and further reading

Magazines/Journals

People Management – fortnightly by subscription
Personnel Today – fortnightly by subscription
Training Manager – fortnightly
Training Officer – monthly

Books/Leaflets

Beech, N and McKenna, E (1995) *The Essence of Human Resource Management*, Prentice Hall, Hemel Hempstead
IPD Guide to Developing an International Personnel Career (1999) CIPD, London
Jones, R (1999) *Getting a Job Abroad: The Handbook for the International Jobseeker: Where the jobs are, how to get them*, How To Books Ltd, Oxford
Qualification Routes (1999) CIPD, London
The Changing Role of the Trainer (1999) CIPD, London
The Grants Register 2000 (1999) Macmillan Reference Ltd, London
Vandevelde, H (1998) *Beyond the CV*, Butterworth-Heinemann, Oxford
Veruki, P (1999) *The 250 Job Interview Questions You'll Most Likely Be Asked... and the Answers That Will Get You Hired!*, Adams Media Corporation, Holbrook MA

9 Useful addresses

As organizations and sites on the Internet change rapidly, there have been relatively few references in the text. However, where a Web site or e-mail address has been provided by the organizations listed below, these have been included.

Association of Graduate Careers Advisory Services (AGCAS)
c/o Careers Advisory Service
University of Nottingham
Cherry Tree Buildings (E)
University Park
Nottingham NG7 2RD
Tel: (0115) 951 3680

The Business Information Service
25 Southampton Buildings
Chancery Lane
London WC2A 1AW
Tel: (020) 7323 7454

Business Technology Education Council (BTEC)
BTEC Central House
Upper Woburn Place
London WC1H 0HH
Tel: (020) 7413 8400

Careers and Occupational Information Centre
Moorfoot
Sheffield
South Yorkshire S1 4PQ
Tel: (01142) 593 002

Central Applications Office
Tower House
Eglinton Street
Galway
Tel: (091) 563 313
Web site: www.indigo.ie\cao\

Chartered Institute of Personnel and Development
CIPD House
Camp Road
London SW19 4UX
Tel: (020) 8971 9000 Fax: (020) 8263 3333
E-mail: ipd@cipd.co.uk
Web site: www.cipd.co.uk

City and Guilds of London Institute (C&G)
1 Giltspur Street
London EC1A 9DD
Tel: (020) 7294 2468

City Business Library
1 Brewers Hall Garden
London EC2V 5BX
Tel: (020) 7638 8215

Commission for Racial Equality
Elliot House
10–12 Allington Street
London SW1E 5EH
Tel: (020) 7828 7022 Fax: (020) 7630 7605
E-mail: info@cre.gov.uk

Useful addresses

Croner CCH Group Ltd
145 London Road
Kingston upon Thames
Surrey KT2 6SR
Tel: (020) 8547 3333 Fax: (020) 8547 2637

Department of Education
Higher Education Section
Block 1
Floor 4
Irish Life Centre
Lower Abbey Street
Dublin 1
Tel: (01) 873 4700 Fax: (01) 872 9003

Department for Education and Employment
Sanctuary Building
Great Smith Street
London SW1P 3BT
Tel: (020) 7925 5000
Web site: www.dfee.gov.uk

Dublin City University,
Glasnevin
Dublin 9
Tel: (01) 704 5000 Fax: (01) 836 0830
E-mail: registrars-office@dcu.ie

Equal Opportunities Commission
Overseas House
Quay Street
Manchester M3 3HN
Tel: (0161) 833 9244 Fax: (0161) 835 1657
E-mail: info@eoc.org.uk

Employment News
Department for Education & Employment
Room E9B
Moorfoot
Sheffield
South Yorkshire S1 4PQ
Tel: (0114) 259 4925 Fax: (0114) 259 4312

Fair Employment Commission for Northern Ireland
Andras House
60 Great Victoria Street
Belfast BT2 7BB
Tel: (01232) 500600 Fax: (01232) 331544

Health and Safety Executive
Sheffield Information Centre
Health and Safety Laboratory
Broad Lane
Sheffield S3 7HQ
Fax: (0114) 2892333

Higher Education Authority
3rd Floor
Marine House
Clanwilliam Court
Dublin 2
Tel: (01) 661 2748 Fax: (01) 661 0492

The Higher Education Careers Services Unit (CSU)
Booth Street East
Manchester M13 9EP
Tel: (0161) 277 5240 Fax: (0161) 277 5250
Web site: http://agcas.csu.ac.uk

Useful addresses

Higher Education Grants Section
Department of Education and Science
Tullamore
Co. Offaly
Eire
Tel: +353 212 75912

Institute for Employment Studies
Mantell Building
Falmer
Brighton BN1 9RF
Tel: (01273) 686 751 Fax: (01273) 690 430
Web site: www.employment-studies.co.uk

The National Association of Educational Guidance for Adults (NAEGA)
1A Hilton Road
Milngauie
East Dunbartonshire G62 7DN
Tel: (0141) 956 5950

The National Centre for Volunteering
Tel: (020) 7520 8900 Fax: (020) 7520 8910
E-mail: Information@thecentre.org.uk
Web site: www.volunteering.org.uk

National Council for Voluntary Organizations
Regent's Wharf
8 All Saints Street
London N1 9RL
Tel: (020) 7713 6161

National Disability Council
Level 4A
Caxton House
Tothill Street
London SW1H 9NA
Tel: (020) 7273 5636 Fax: (020) 7273 5929
Web site: www.disability-council.gov.uk

The National Extension College
18 Brooklands Avenue
Cambridge CB2 2HN
Tel: (01223) 316 644

National Union of Students
461 Holloway Road
London N7 6LJ
Tel: (020) 7272 8900

National University of Ireland, Cork (UCC)
Tel: (021) 276 871 Fax: (021) 271 568
E-mail: downtown@sec.ucc.ie

National University of Ireland, Dublin (UCD)
Belfield
Dublin 4
Tel: (01) 269 3244 Fax:(01) 269 4409
Web site: www.ucd.ie

National University of Ireland, Galway (UCG)
Tel: (091) 24411 Fax: (091) 524 411
Web site: www.ucg.ie

National University of Ireland, Maynooth
Co. Kildare.
Tel: (01) 628 5222 Fax: (01) 628 9063
Web site: www.may.ie

The Open College
St Paul's
781 Wilmslow Road
Didsbury
Manchester M20 3BZ
Tel: (0161) 434 0007

Further information

The Open University
Central Enquiry Service
PO Box 200
Milton Keynes MK7 6YZ
Tel: (01908) 653231 Fax: (01908) 654806
Web site: www.open.ac.uk

People Management
17–18 Britton Street
London EC1M 5NQ
Tel: (020) 7880 6200 Fax: (020) 7336 7635

Personnel Today
Reed Business Publishing Ltd
Quadrant House
The Quadrant
Sutton
Surrey SM2 5AS
Tel: (020) 8652 3944 Fax: (020) 8652 8805
Web site: www.reedbusiness.com/personnel.htm

Pitmans Examination Institute (PEI)
1 Giltspur Street
London EC1A 9DD
Tel: (020) 7294 2471

RSA Examination Board
Westwood Way
Coventry CV4 8HS
Tel: (01203) 470 033

Scottish Council for Voluntary Organizations
18–19 Claremont Crescent
Edinburgh EH7 4QD
Tel: (0131) 556 3882

Scottish Qualifications Authority (SQA)
Hanover House
24 Douglas Street
Glasgow G2 7NQ
Tel: (0141) 248 7900

Training Management
Inside Communications
9 White Lion Street
London N1 9XJ
Tel: (020) 7837 8727 Fax: (020) 7837 7064

Training Officer
Lloyds House
18 Lloyd Street
Manchester M2 5WA
Tel: (0161) 832 6541 Fax: (0161) 832 8129

Universities and Colleges Admission Service (UCAS)
Rosehill
New Barn Lane
Cheltenham
Gloucestershire GL52 3LZ.
Tel: (01242) 222 444

University of Dublin, Trinity College
Dublin 2
Tel: (01) 677 2941 Fax: (01) 677 2694
Web site: www.tcd.ie

University of Limerick
Plassey Technological Park
Limerick
Tel: (061) 333 644 Fax: (061) 330 316
Web site: www.ul.ie

Index

Association of Graduate Careers Advisory Services (AGCAS) 58

benefits, pay and pensions 4, 29–32
Business and Technology Education Council (BTEC) 45, 67

Certificate in Personnel Practice (CPP) 68–69
Certificate in Training Practice (CTP) 68–69
charities 11–12
City & Guilds of London Institute (C&G) 67
colleges and universities
 applying to 55–56
 distance learning 54–55
 financial help 56–57
 HRM specialists 45–47
 post-graduate education 69–73
 professional education 66
 selecting for HRM career 53–55
communication
 employee/industrial relations 19–22
consultancies 43–44
 future prospects 77–78
 specialization in HRM areas 34
cultural difference
 organizational development 37

distance learning 54–55
 certificate level 68

employees
 changing to HRM from another career 50–51, 52, 62–63
 HRM role 13–14, 19–22
 job hunting for HRM positions 57–60

 returning to work 52 *see also* industrial relations
equal opportunities 4
 HRM role 25–28
 'managing diversity' 27–28

health and safety 4
 HRM role 28–29
 as industrial relations issue 21, 29
Higher National Diploma (HND) 45
human resource development (HRD) 3
human resource management (HRM)
 academic careers 45–47
 career planning 48
 changing from another career 50–51, 52
 consultancies 34, 43–44
 future prospects 75–78
 generalists 3, 13–14
 job hunting 57–60
 management development 35–36
 outsourced by organizations 41–43
 personal development 61
 roles and responsibilities 3–4, 39–40
 school and university possibilities 49–50
 self-evaluation 1–2
 specialization 32–39, 44–45
 tips for self-development 48
 typical professional 6
 variety of careers 5–6
human resource planning 4
 importance and approaches 17–19

industrial relations 4
 health and safety issues 21, 29
 HRM role 13–14, 19–22

91

Index

information technology
  software design/development   4, 37–39
Institute of Personnel and Development (IPD)   4–5, 6, 45
  continuous profession development programmes   75
  membership benefits   50, 54
  routes to qualifications   63–65, 65–67
interviewing skills   15
Investors in People (IIP)   34, 44

job hunting   57–60

law
  contracts   8–9
  equal opportunities   25
  international   4, 44–45
  specialization   44–45

management
  development   4, 35–36
  equal opportunities   27–28
  post-graduate education   69–71

National Vocational Qualifications (NVQs) assessment   67

occupational areas *see* employees; recruitment and selection
occupational psychologist   13, 15
Open University   55
organizations
  cultural differences   37
  development   4, 36–37
  outsourcing HRM   41–43, 77
  private, public and voluntary sectors   9–12
  size   7–9
  trends and future developments in HRM   75–78

pay *see* benefits, pay and pensions
pensions *see* benefits, pay and pensions
Pitman Examination Institute   67
private and public sectors   9–10

professionalism   4–5

Qualification Guidelines (IPD)   66
qualifications
  academic career   45–47
  assessment against NVQs/SVQs   67
  basic office and administrative skills   62
  certificate level   68–69
  consultants   44
  continuing development   73–74
  guidelines from IPD   66
  linked to IPD   63–65
  post-graduate education   69–73
  professional assessment   66–67
  routes to   65–67
  school and university career planning   49–50, 52–53
  selecting learning centres/institutions   53–55 *see also* colleges and universities
  versus experience   62–64

recruitment and selection   4
  contracts   8–9
  HRM role in   14–17
  job descriptions   8
  post-graduate education   71–72
rewards *see* benefits, pay and pensions
RSA Examinations Board   67

Scottish Qualifications Authority   67
Scottish Vocational Qualifications (SVQs)   67
software design/development   4
  HRM specialists   37–39

trade unions *see* industrial relations
training and development
  HRM role   22–25
  as part of employee relations   21
Training and Enterprise Councils (TECs)   44

Universities and Colleges Admission Service (UCAS)   55